2,000
CHINESE CHARACTERS
A Comparison Guide to
Traditional and Simplified Forms

汉字繁简对照表

LONG RIVER PRESS

San Francisco

First Edition 2004
Copyright © Long River Press 2004
ISBN 1-59265-035-X

Long River Press
360 Swift Ave, Unit 48
South San Francisco, CA 94080
www.longriverpress.com

Printed in China

Contents

Introduction

The Chinese written language has evolved over the centuries from simple pictographic inscriptions into highly complex characters, many of which are extremely difficult to master. These are known as traditional characters.

To foster and accelerate language learning and recognition of written Chinese characters, a simplified form of written Chinese was developed. By 1986, a complete list of the simplified Chinese characters yielded a total of 2,235 characters. Thus, the simplified characters comprise roughly XX% of the total Chinese written language.

To help those new to the Chinese language, as well as those who may have already learned to read traditional Chinese characters, this book provides useful comparisons between traditional and simplified characters. Also featured are a selection of indices, such as a pinyin index; a zhuyin index; and a stroke index. In addition, a comparative table of romanization, together with a list of simplified radicals, is also provided for reference and ease-of-use.

Simplified Chinese characters are now widely used in the People's Republic of China and in the majority of Chinese language programs in colleges and universities both in China and abroad. Simplified characters are used in book publishing, newspapers, magazines, official publications and documents, television and movie subtitles, and virtually all aspects of everyday life. Traditional characters are still commonly used in Taiwan and Hong Kong, and can be found in many overseas Chinese communities throughout the world.

Traditional Chinese characters can still be seen in China today. Because of their aesthetic appeal, they remain unchanged in classical literature, poetry, and in notable historical texts. Traditional characters are also widely encountered in painting and calligraphic work, and seal carving.

Romanization Systems of Chinese Characters

汉字拼音符号
对 照 表

Pinyin	Wade-Giles	Yale	Zhuyin

A

a	a	a	ㄚ
ai	ai	ai	ㄞ
an	an	an	ㄢ
ang	ang	ang	ㄤ
ao	ao	au	ㄠ

B

ba	pa	ba	ㄅㄚ
bai	pai	bai	ㄅㄞ
ban	pan	ban	ㄅㄢ
bang	pang	bang	ㄅㄤ
bao	pao	bau	ㄅㄠ
bei	pei	bei	ㄅㄟ
ben	pen	ben	ㄅㄣ
beng	peng	beng	ㄅㄥ
bi	pi	bi	ㄅㄧ
bian	pien	byan	ㄅㄧㄢ
biao	piao	byau	ㄅㄧㄠ
bie	pieh	bye	ㄅㄧㄝ
bin	pin	bin	ㄅㄧㄣ
bing	ping	bing	ㄅㄧㄥ
bo	po	bwo	ㄅㄛ
bu	pu	bu	ㄅㄨ

C

ca	ts'a	tsa	ㄘㄚ
cai	ts'ai	tsai	ㄘㄞ
can	ts'an	tsan	ㄘㄢ
cang	ts'ang	tsang	ㄘㄤ
cao	ts'ao	tau	ㄘㄠ
ce	ts'e	tse	ㄘㄜ
cei	ts'ei	tsei	ㄘㄟ
cen	ts'en	tsen	ㄘㄣ
ceng	ts'eng	tseng	ㄘㄥ
cha	ch'a	cha	ㄔㄚ
chai	ch'ai	chai	ㄔㄞ
chan	ch'an	chan	ㄔㄢ
chang	ch'ang	chang	ㄔㄤ
chao	ch'ao	chau	ㄔㄠ
che	ch'e	che	ㄔㄜ
chen	ch'en	chen	ㄔㄣ
cheng	ch'eng	cheng	ㄔㄥ
chi	ch'ih	chr	ㄔ
chong	ch'ung	chung	ㄔㄨㄥ
chou	ch'ou	chou	ㄔㄡ
chu	ch'u	chu	ㄔㄨ
chua	ch'ua	chwa	ㄔㄨㄚ
chuai	ch'uai	chwai	ㄔㄨㄞ
chuan	ch'uan	chwan	ㄔㄨㄢ
chuang	ch'uang	chwang	ㄔㄨㄤ
chui	ch'ui	chwei	ㄔㄨㄟ
chun	ch'un	chwun	ㄔㄨㄣ
chuo	ch'o	chwo	ㄔㄨㄛ

ci	tz'u	tsz	ㄘ
cong	ts'ung	tsung	ㄘㄨㄥ
cou	ts'ou	tsou	ㄘㄡ
cu	ts'u	tsu	ㄘㄨ
cuan	ts'uan	tswan	ㄘㄨㄢ
cui	ts'ui	tswei	ㄘㄨㄟ
cun	ts'un	tswun	ㄘㄨㄣ
cuo	ts'o	tswo	ㄘㄨㄛ

D

da	ta	da	ㄉㄚ
dai	tai	dai	ㄉㄞ
dan	tan	dan	ㄉㄢ
dang	tang	dang	ㄉㄤ
dao	tao	dau	ㄉㄠ
de	te	de	ㄉㄜ
dei	tei	dei	ㄉㄟ
den	ten	den	ㄉㄣ
deng	teng	deng	ㄉㄥ
di	ti	di	ㄉㄧ
dia	tia	dya	ㄉㄧㄚ
dian	tien	dyan	ㄉㄧㄢ
diao	tiao	dyau	ㄉㄧㄠ
die	tieh	dye	ㄉㄧㄝ
ding	ting	ding	ㄉㄧㄥ
diu	tiu	dyou	ㄉㄧㄡ
dong	tung	dung	ㄉㄨㄥ
dou	tou	dou	ㄉㄡ
du	tu	du	ㄉㄨ
duan	tuan	dwan	ㄉㄨㄢ
dui	tui	dwei	ㄉㄨㄟ

| dun | tun | dwun | ㄉㄨㄣ |
| duo | to | dwo | ㄉㄨㄛ |

E

e	e, o	e	ㄜ
en	en	en	ㄣ
eng	eng	eng	ㄥ
er	erh	er	ㄦ

F

fa	fa	fa	ㄈㄚ
fan	fan	fan	ㄈㄢ
fang	fang	fang	ㄈㄤ
fei	fei	fei	ㄈㄟ
fen	fen	fen	ㄈㄣ
feng	feng	feng	ㄈㄥ
fiao	fiao	fyao	ㄈㄧㄠ
fo	fo	fwo	ㄈㄛ
fou	fou	fou	ㄈㄡ
fu	fu	fu	ㄈㄨ

G

ga	ka	ga	ㄍㄚ
gai	kai	gai	ㄍㄞ
gan	kan	gan	ㄍㄢ
gang	kang	gang	ㄍㄤ
gao	kao	gau	ㄍㄠ
ge	ko, ke	ge	ㄍㄜ
gei	kei	gei	ㄍㄟ
gen	ken	gen	ㄍㄣ
geng	keng	geng	ㄍㄥ

gong	kung	gung	ㄍㄨㄥ
gou	kou	gou	ㄍㄡ
gu	ku	gu	ㄍㄨ
gua	kua	gwa	ㄍㄨㄚ
guai	kuai	gwai	ㄍㄨㄞ
guan	kuan	gwan	ㄍㄨㄢ
guang	kuang	gwang	ㄍㄨㄤ
gui	kuei	gwei	ㄍㄨㄟ
gun	kun	gwun	ㄍㄨㄣ
guo	kuo	gwo	ㄍㄨㄛ

H

ha	ha	ha	ㄏㄚ
hai	hai	hai	ㄏㄞ
han	han	han	ㄏㄢ
hang	hang	hang	ㄏㄤ
hao	hao	hau	ㄏㄠ
he	he	he	ㄏㄜ
hei	hei	hei	ㄏㄟ
hen	hen	hen	ㄏㄣ
hm	hm	hm	ㄏㄇ
hng	hng	hng	ㄏㄫ
heng	heng	heng	ㄏㄥ
hong	hung	hung	ㄏㄨㄥ
hou	hou	hou	ㄏㄡ
hu	hu	hu	ㄏㄨ
hua	hua	hwa	ㄏㄨㄚ
huai	huai	hwai	ㄏㄨㄞ
huan	huan	hwan	ㄏㄨㄢ
huang	huang	hwang	ㄏㄨㄤ
hui	hui	hui	ㄏㄨㄟ

hun	hun	hwun	ㄏㄨㄣ
huo	huo	hwo	ㄏㄨㄛ

J

ji	chi	ji	ㄐㄧ
jia	chia	jya	ㄐㄧㄚ
jian	chien	jyan	ㄐㄧㄢ
jiang	chiang	yjang	ㄐㄧㄤ
jiao	chiao	jyao	ㄐㄧㄠ
jie	chieh	jye	ㄐㄧㄝ
jin	chin	jin	ㄐㄧㄣ
jing	ching	jing	ㄐㄧㄥ
jiong	chiung	jyung	ㄐㄩㄥ
jiu	chiu	jyou	ㄐㄧㄡ
ju	chü	jyu	ㄐㄩ
juan	chüan	jywan	ㄐㄩㄢ
jue	chüeh	jywe	ㄐㄩㄝ
jun	chün	jyun	ㄐㄩㄣ

K

ka	k'a	ka	ㄎㄚ
kai	k'ai	kai	ㄎㄞ
kan	k'an	kan	ㄎㄢ
kang	k'ang	kang	ㄎㄤ
kao	k'ao	kau	ㄎㄠ
ke	k'e, k'o	ke	ㄎㄜ
kei	k'ei	kei	ㄎㄟ
ken	k'en	ken	ㄎㄣ
keng	k'eng	keng	ㄎㄥ
kong	k'ong	kong	ㄎㄨㄥ
kou	k'ou	kou	ㄎㄡ

ku	k'u	ku	ㄎㄨ
kua	k'ua	kwa	ㄎㄨㄚ
kuai	k'uai	kwai	ㄎㄨㄞ
kuan	k'uan	kwan	ㄎㄨㄢ
kuang	k'uang	kwang	ㄎㄨㄤ
kui	k'uei	kwei	ㄎㄨㄟ
kun	k'un	kwun	ㄎㄨㄣ
kuo	k'uo	kwo	ㄎㄨㄛ

L

la	la	la	ㄌㄚ
lai	lai	lai	ㄌㄞ
lan	lan	lan	ㄌㄢ
lang	lang	lang	ㄌㄤ
lao	lao	lau	ㄌㄠ
le	le	le	ㄌㄜ
lei	lei	lei	ㄌㄟ
leng	leng	leng	ㄌㄥ
li	li	li	ㄌㄧ
lia	lia	lya	ㄌㄧㄚ
lian	lien	lyan	ㄌㄧㄢ
liang	liang	lyang	ㄌㄧㄤ
liao	liao	lyau	ㄌㄧㄠ
lie	lieh	lye	ㄌㄧㄝ
lin	lin	lin	ㄌㄧㄣ
ling	ling	ling	ㄌㄧㄥ
liu	liu	lyou	ㄌㄧㄡ
lo	lo	lwo	ㄌㄛ
long	lung	lung	ㄌㄨㄥ
lou	lou	lou	ㄌㄡ
lu	lu	lu	ㄌㄨ

lü	lü	lyu	ㄌㄩ
luan	luan	lwan	ㄌㄨㄢ
lüe	lüeh	lywe	ㄌㄩㄝ
lun	lun, lün	lwun	ㄌㄨㄣ
luo	lo	lwo	ㄌㄨㄛ

M

m	m	m	ㄇ
ma	ma	ma	ㄇㄚ
mai	mai	mai	ㄇㄞ
man	man	man	ㄇㄢ
mang	mang	mang	ㄇㄤ
mao	mao	mau	ㄇㄠ
me	me	me	ㄇㄜ
mei	mei	mei	ㄇㄟ
men	men	men	ㄇㄣ
meng	meng	meng	ㄇㄥ
mi	mi	mi	ㄇㄧ
mian	mien	myan	ㄇㄧㄢ
miao	miao	myau	ㄇㄧㄠ
mie	mieh	mye	ㄇㄧㄝ
min	min	min	ㄇㄧㄣ
ming	ming	ming	ㄇㄧㄥ
miu	miu	myou	ㄇㄧㄡ
mo	mo	mwo	ㄇㄛ
mou	mou	mou	ㄇㄡ
mu	mu	mu	ㄇㄨ

N

n	n	n	ㄋ
na	na	na	ㄋㄚ

nai	nai	nai	ㄋㄞ
nan	nan	nan	ㄋㄢ
nang	nang	nang	ㄋㄤ
nao	nao	nau	ㄋㄠ
ne	ne	ne	ㄋㄜ
nei	nei	nei	ㄋㄟ
nen	nen	nen	ㄋㄣ
neng	neng	neng	ㄋㄥ
ng	ng	ng	ㄫ
ni	ni	ni	ㄋㄧ
nian	nien	nyan	ㄋㄧㄢ
niang	niang	nyang	ㄋㄧㄤ
niao	niao	nyau	ㄋㄧㄠ
nie	nieh	nye	ㄋㄧㄝ
nin	nin	nin	ㄋㄧㄣ
ning	ning	ning	ㄋㄧㄥ
niu	niu	nyou	ㄋㄧㄡ
nong	nung	nung	ㄋㄧㄥ
nou	nou	nou	ㄋㄡ
nu	nu	nu	ㄋㄨ
nü	nü	nyu	ㄋㄩ
nuan	nuan	nwan	ㄋㄨㄢ
nüe	nüeh	nywe	ㄋㄩㄝ
nun	nun	nwun	ㄋㄨㄣ
nuo	nuo	nwo	ㄋㄨㄛ

O

o	o	o	ㄛ
ou	ou	ou	ㄡ

P

pa	p'a	pa	ㄆㄚ
pai	p'ai	pai	ㄆㄞ
pan	p'an	pan	ㄆㄢ
pang	p'ang	pang	ㄆㄤ
pao	p'ao	pau	ㄆㄠ
pei	p'ei	pei	ㄆㄟ
pen	p'en	pen	ㄆㄣ
peng	p'eng	peng	ㄆㄥ
pi	p'i	pi	ㄆㄧ
pian	p'ien	pyan	ㄆㄧㄢ
piao	p'iao	pyau	ㄆㄧㄠ
pie	p'ieh	pye	ㄆㄧㄝ
pin	p'in	pin	ㄆㄧㄣ
ping	p'ing	ping	ㄆㄧㄥ
po	p'o	pwo	ㄆㄛ
pou	p'ou	pou	ㄆㄡ
pu	p'u	pu	ㄆㄨ

Q

qi	ch'i	chi	ㄑㄧ
qia	ch'ia	chya	ㄑㄧㄚ
qian	ch'ien	chyan	ㄑㄧㄢ
qiang	ch'iang	chyang	ㄑㄧㄤ
qiao	ch'iao	chyau	ㄑㄧㄠ
qie	ch'ieh	chye	ㄑㄧㄝ
qin	ch'in	chin	ㄑㄧㄣ
qing	ch'ing	ching	ㄑㄧㄥ
qiong	ch'iung	chyung	ㄑㄩㄥ
qiu	ch'iu	chyou	ㄑㄧㄡ

qu	ch'ü	chyu	ㄑㄩ
quan	ch'üan	chywan	ㄑㄩㄢ
que	ch'üeh	chywe	ㄑㄩㄝ
qun	ch'ün	chyun	ㄑㄩㄣ

R

ran	jan	ran	ㄖㄢ
rang	jang	rang	ㄖㄤ
rao	jao	rau	ㄖㄠ
re	je	re	ㄖㄜ
ren	jen	ren	ㄖㄣ
reng	jeng	reng	ㄖㄥ
ri	jih	r	ㄖ
rong	jung	rung	ㄖㄨㄥ
rou	jou	rou	ㄖㄡ
ru	ju	ru	ㄖㄨ
rua	jua	rwa	ㄖㄨㄚ
ruan	juan	rwan	ㄖㄨㄢ
rui	jui	rwei	ㄖㄨㄟ
run	jun	rwun	ㄖㄨㄣ
ruo	jo	rwo	ㄖㄨㄛ

S

sa	sa	sa	ㄙㄚ
sai	sai	sai	ㄙㄞ
san	san	san	ㄙㄢ
sang	sang	sang	ㄙㄤ
sao	sao	sau	ㄙㄠ
se	se	se	ㄙㄜ
sen	sen	sen	ㄙㄣ
seng	seng	seng	ㄙㄥ

sha	sha	sha	ㄕㄚ
shai	shai	shai	ㄕㄞ
shan	shan	shan	ㄕㄢ
shang	shang	shang	ㄕㄤ
shao	shao	shau	ㄕㄠ
she	she	she	ㄕㄜ
shei	shei	shei	ㄕㄟ
shen	shen	shen	ㄕㄣ
sheng	sheng	sheng	ㄕㄥ
shi	shih	shr	ㄕ
shou	shou	shou	ㄕㄡ
shu	shu	shu	ㄕㄨ
shua	shua	shwa	ㄕㄨㄚ
shuai	shuai	shwai	ㄕㄨㄞ
shuan	shuan	shwan	ㄕㄨㄢ
shuang	shuang	shwang	ㄕㄨㄤ
shui	shui	shwei	ㄕㄨㄟ
shun	shun	shwun	ㄕㄨㄣ
shuo	shuo	shwo	ㄕㄨㄛ
si	ssu, szu	sz	ㄙ
song	sung	sung	ㄙㄨㄥ
sou	sou	sou	ㄙㄡ
su	su	su	ㄙㄨ
suan	suan	swan	ㄙㄨㄢ
sui	sui	swei	ㄙㄨㄟ
sun	sun	swun	ㄙㄨㄣ
suo	so	swo	ㄙㄨㄛ

T

ta	t'a	ta	ㄊㄚ
tai	t'ai	tai	ㄊㄞ

tan	t'an	tan	ㄊㄢ
tang	t'ang	tang	ㄊㄤ
tao	t'ao	tao	ㄊㄠ
te	t'e	te	ㄊㄜ
tei	t'ei	tei	ㄊㄟ
teng	t'eng	teng	ㄊㄥ
ti	t'i	ti	ㄊㄧ
tian	t'ien	tyan	ㄊㄧㄢ
tiao	t'iao	tyau	ㄊㄧㄠ
tie	t'ieh	tye	ㄊㄧㄝ
ting	t'ing	ting	ㄊㄧㄥ
tong	t'ung	tung	ㄊㄨㄥ
tou	t'ou	tou	ㄊㄡ
tu	t'u	tu	ㄊㄨ
tuan	t'uan	twan	ㄊㄨㄢ
tui	t'ui	twei	ㄊㄨㄟ
tun	t'un	twun	ㄊㄨㄣ
tuo	t'o	two	ㄊㄨㄛ

W

wa	wa	wa	ㄨㄚ
wai	wai	wai	ㄨㄞ
wan	wan	wan	ㄨㄢ
wang	wang	wang	ㄨㄤ
wei	wei	wei	ㄨㄟ
wen	wen	wen	ㄨㄣ
weng	weng	weng	ㄨㄥ
wo	wo	wo	ㄨㄛ
wu	wu	wu	ㄨ

X

xi	hsi	syi	ㄒㄧ
xia	hsia	sya	ㄒㄧㄚ
xian	hsien	syan	ㄒㄧㄢ
xiang	hsiang	syang	ㄒㄧㄤ
xiao	hsiao	syau	ㄒㄧㄠ
xie	hsieh	sye	ㄒㄧㄝ
xin	hsin	syin	ㄒㄧㄣ
xing	hsing	sying	ㄒㄧㄥ
xiong	hsiung	syung	ㄒㄩㄥ
xiu	hsiu	syou	ㄒㄧㄡ
xu	hsü	syu	ㄒㄩ
xuan	hsüan	sywan	ㄒㄩㄢ
xue	hsüeh	sywe	ㄒㄩㄝ
xun	hsün	syun	ㄒㄩㄣ

Y

ya	ya	ya	ㄧㄚ
yai	yai	yai	ㄧㄞ
yan	yen	yan	ㄧㄢ
yang	yang	yang	ㄧㄤ
yao	yao	yau	ㄧㄠ
ye	yeh	ye	ㄧㄝ
yi	yi, i	yi	ㄧ
yin	yin	yin	ㄧㄣ
ying	ying	ying	ㄧㄥ
yong	yung	yung	ㄩㄥ
you	yu	you	ㄧㄡ
yu	yü	yu	ㄩ
yuan	yüan	ywan	ㄩㄢ

yue	yüeh	ywe	ㄩ ㄝ
yun	yün	yun	ㄩ ㄣ

Z

za	tsa	dza	ㄗ ㄚ
zai	tsai	dzai	ㄗ ㄞ
zan	tsan	dzan	ㄗ ㄢ
zang	tsang	dzang	ㄗ ㄤ
zao	tsao	dzau	ㄗ ㄠ
ze	tse	dze	ㄗ ㄜ
zei	tsei	dzei	ㄗ ㄟ
zen	tsen	dzen	ㄗ ㄣ
zeng	tseng	dzeng	ㄗ ㄥ
zha	cha	ja	ㄓ ㄚ
zhai	chai	jai	ㄓ ㄞ
zhan	chan	jan	ㄓ ㄢ
zhang	chang	jang	ㄓ ㄤ
zhao	chao	jau	ㄓ ㄠ
zhe	che	je	ㄓ ㄜ
zhei	chei	jei	ㄓ ㄟ
zhen	chen	jen	ㄓ ㄣ
zheng	cheng	jeng	ㄓ ㄥ
zhi	chih	jr	ㄓ
zhong	chung	jung	ㄓ ㄨ ㄥ
zhou	chou	jou	ㄓ ㄡ
zhu	chu	ju	ㄓ ㄨ
zhua	chua	jwa	ㄓ ㄨ ㄚ
zhuai	chuai	jwai	ㄓ ㄨ ㄞ
zhuan	chuan	jwan	ㄓ ㄨ ㄢ
zhuang	chuang	jwang	ㄓ ㄨ ㄤ
zhui	chui	jwei	ㄓ ㄨ ㄟ

zhun	chun	jwun	ㄓㄨㄣ
zhuo	cho	jwo	ㄓㄨㄛ
zi	tzu	dz	ㄗ
zong	tsung	dzung	ㄗㄨㄥ
zou	tsou	dzou	ㄗㄡ
zu	tsu	dzu	ㄗㄨ
zuan	tsuan	dzwan	ㄗㄨㄢ
zui	tsui	dzwei	ㄗㄨㄟ
zun	tsun	dzwun	ㄗㄨㄣ
zuo	tso	dzwo	ㄗㄨㄛ

From Simplified to Traditional Characters

简 繁 对 照

Radicals
简化偏旁

A

爱 – 愛

B

罢 – 罷
贝 – 貝
备 – 備
笔 – 筆
毕 – 畢
边 – 邊
宾 – 賓

C

参 – 參
仓 – 倉
产 – 産
尝 – 嘗
长 – 長
车 – 車
齿 – 齒
虫 – 蟲
刍 – 芻
从 – 從
窜 – 竄

D

达 – 達
带 – 帶
单 – 單
当 – 當
　 – 噹
党 – 黨
东 – 東
动 – 動
断 – 斷
对 – 對
队 – 隊

E

尔 – 爾

F

发 – 發
　 – 髮
丰 – 豐
风 – 風

G

冈 – 岡

广 – 廣
归 – 歸
龟 – 龜
国 – 國
过 – 過

H

华 – 華
画 – 畫
汇 – 匯
　 – 彙
会 – 會

J

几 – 幾
夹 – 夾
戋 – 戔
监 – 監
荐 – 薦
见 – 見
将 – 將
节 – 節
进 – 進
尽 – 盡
　 – 儘

举 – 舉
车 – 車

K

壳 – 殼
会 – 會

L

来 – 來
乐 – 樂
离 – 離
丽 – 麗
历 – 歷
　 – 曆
两 – 兩
灵 – 靈
刘 – 劉
龙 – 龍
娄 – 婁
卢 – 盧
卤 – 鹵
　 – 滷
虏 – 虜
录 – 録
虑 – 慮

23

仑 – 侖
罗 – 羅
　　囉

M

马 – 馬
买 – 買
卖 – 賣
麦 – 麥
门 – 門
黾 – 黽

N

难 – 難
鸟 – 鳥
聂 – 聶
宁 – 寧
农 – 農

O

区 – 區

Q

齐 – 齊
岂 – 豈
气 – 氣

佥 – 僉
迁 – 遷
乔 – 喬
壳 – 殼
亲 – 親
穷 – 窮
区 – 區

S

啬 – 嗇
杀 – 殺
参 – 參
审 – 審
圣 – 聖
师 – 師
时 – 時
寿 – 壽
属 – 屬
双 – 雙
肃 – 肅
岁 – 歲
孙 – 孫

T

条 – 條

W

万 – 萬

为 – 爲
韦 – 韋
乌 – 烏
无 – 無

X

献 – 獻
乡 – 鄉
写 – 寫
寻 – 尋

Y

亚 – 亞
严 – 嚴
厌 – 厭
尧 – 堯
页 – 頁
业 – 業
义 – 義
艺 – 藝
阴 – 陰
隐 – 隱
犹 – 猶
鱼 – 魚
与 – 與

乐 – 樂
云 – 雲

Z

长 – 長
郑 – 鄭
执 – 執
质 – 質
专 – 專

简化偏旁

讠 – 言
饣 – 食
昜 – 昜
纟 – 糸
収 – 臤
䒑 – 竹
临 – 臨
只 – 哉
钅 – 金
兴 – 與
罕 – 罨
巠 – 巠
亦 – 戀
咼 – 咼

Pinyin Index
汉语拼音索引

缤 – 繽
镔 – 鑌
濒 – 瀕
鬓 – 鬢
摈 – 擯
殡 – 殯
膑 – 臏
髌 – 髕

bing
槟 – 檳
饼 – 餅

bo
饽 – 餑
钵 – 鉢
拨 – 撥
鹁 – 鵓
馎 – 餺
钹 – 鈸
驳 – 駁
铂 – 鉑
卜 – 蔔

bu
补 – 補
钚 – 鈈

C

cai
才 – 纔
财 – 財

can
参 – 參
骖 – 驂

蚕 – 蠶
惭 – 慚
残 – 殘
惨 – 慘
穇 – 穇
灿 – 燦

cang
仓 – 倉
沧 – 滄
苍 – 蒼
伧 – 傖
鸧 – 鶬
舱 – 艙

ce
测 – 測
恻 – 惻
厕 – 厠
侧 – 側

cen
参 – 參

ceng
层 – 層

cha
馇 – 餷
锸 – 鍤
镲 – 鑔
诧 – 詫

chai
钗 – 釵
侪 – 儕
虿 – 蠆

chan
搀 – 攙
掺 – 摻
缠 – 纏
禅 – 禪
蝉 – 蟬
婵 – 嬋
谗 – 讒
馋 – 饞
产 – 產
浐 – 滻
铲 – 鏟
蒇 – 蕆
阐 – 闡
辗 – 幝
谄 – 諂
颤 – 顫
忏 – 懺
划 – 剗

chang
伥 – 倀
阊 – 閶
鲳 – 鯧
尝 – 嘗
偿 – 償
鲿 – 鱨
长 – 長
肠 – 腸
场 – 場
厂 – 廠
怅 – 悵

畅 – 暢

chao
钞 – 鈔

che
车 – 車
砗 – 硨
彻 – 徹

chen
谌 – 諶
尘 – 塵
陈 – 陳
碜 – 磣
榇 – 櫬
衬 – 襯
谶 – 讖
称 – 稱
龀 – 齔

cheng
柽 – 檉
蛏 – 蟶
铛 – 鐺
桢 – 檉
称 – 稱
枨 – 棖
诚 – 誠
惩 – 懲
骋 – 騁

chi
鸱 – 鴟
迟 – 遲
驰 – 馳

齿 – 齒	铡 – 鍘	**cuan**	惮 – 憚
炽 – 熾	**chuang**	撺 – 攛	瘅 – 癉
饬 – 飭	疮 – 瘡	蹿 – 躥	弹 – 彈
chong	闯 – 闖	镩 – 鑹	诞 – 誕
冲 – 衝	怆 – 愴	攒 – 攢	**dang**
虫 – 蟲	创 – 創	窜 – 竄	裆 – 襠
宠 – 寵	**chui**	**cui**	铛 – 鐺
铳 – 銃	锤 – 錘	缞 – 縗	当 – 當
chou	**chun**	**cuo**	噹
绌 – 紬	䲟 – 鰆	嵯 – 嵯	党 – 黨
畴 – 疇	鹑 – 鶉	错 – 錯	谠 – 讜
筹 – 籌	纯 – 純	锉 – 銼	挡 – 擋
踌 – 躊	莼 – 蓴	**D**	档 – 檔
俦 – 儔	**chuo**	**da**	砀 – 碭
雠 – 讎	绰 – 綽	达 – 達	荡 – 蕩
绸 – 綢	龊 – 齪	哒 – 噠	**dao**
丑 – 醜	辍 – 輟	鞑 – 韃	刀 – 刅
chu	**ci**	**dai**	祷 – 禱
出 – 齣	鹚 – 鷀	贷 – 貸	岛 – 島
锄 – 鋤	辞 – 辭	给 – 給	捣 – 搗
刍 – 芻	词 – 詞	带 – 帶	导 – 導
雏 – 雛	赐 – 賜	靆 – 靆	**de**
储 – 儲	**cong**	**dan**	锝 – 鍀
础 – 礎	聪 – 聰	单 – 單	**deng**
处 – 處	骢 – 驄	担 – 擔	灯 – 燈
绌 – 絀	枞 – 樅	殚 – 殫	镫 – 鐙
触 – 觸	苁 – 蓯	箪 – 簞	邓 – 鄧
chuai	从 – 從	郸 – 鄲	**di**
闯 – 闖	丛 – 叢	掸 – 撣	镝 – 鏑
chuan	**cou**	胆 – 膽	觌 – 覿
传 – 傳	辏 – 輳	赕 – 賧	籴 – 糴

敌 – 敵
涤 – 滌
诋 – 詆
谛 – 諦
缔 – 締
递 – 遞

dian

颠 – 顛
癫 – 癲
巅 – 巔
点 – 點
淀 – 澱
垫 – 墊
电 – 電
钿 – 鈿

diao

鲷 – 鯛
铫 – 銚
锦 – 銱
窎 – 窵
钓 – 釣
调 – 調

die

谍 – 諜
鲽 – 鰈
绖 – 絰
迭 – 叠

ding

钉 – 釘
顶 – 頂
订 – 訂

锭 – 錠

diu

铥 – 銩

dong

东 – 東
鸫 – 鶇
岽 – 崬
冬 – 鼕
动 – 動
冻 – 凍
栋 – 棟
胨 – 腖

dou

铘 – 鈄
斗 – 鬥
窦 – 竇

du

读 – 讀
渎 – 瀆
椟 – 櫝
黩 – 黷
犊 – 犢
牍 – 牘
独 – 獨
赌 – 賭
笃 – 篤
镀 – 鍍

duan

断 – 斷
锻 – 鍛
缎 – 緞

簖 – 籪

dui

怼 – 懟
对 – 對
队 – 隊

dun

吨 – 噸
镦 – 鐓
趸 – 躉
钝 – 鈍
顿 – 頓

duo

夺 – 奪
铎 – 鐸
驮 – 馱
堕 – 墮
饳 – 飿

E

e

额 – 額
锇 – 鋨
鹅 – 鵝
讹 – 訛
恶 – 惡
噁
垩 – 堊
轭 – 軛
谔 – 諤
鹗 – 鶚
鳄 – 鱷
锷 – 鍔

饿 – 餓

ê

诶 – 誒

er

儿 – 兒
鸸 – 鴯
饵 – 餌
铒 – 鉺
尔 – 爾
迩 – 邇
贰 – 貳

F

fa

发 – 發
髮
罚 – 罰
阀 – 閥

fan

烦 – 煩
矾 – 礬
钒 – 釩
贩 – 販
饭 – 飯
范 – 範

fang

钫 – 鈁
鲂 – 魴
访 – 訪
纺 – 紡

fei

绯 – 緋

鲱 – 鯡	辐 – 輻	赶 – 趕	**gong**
飞 – 飛	鞁 – 鞁	赣 – 贛	龚 – 龔
诽 – 誹	绂 – 紱	绀 – 紺	巩 – 鞏
废 – 廢	凫 – 鳧	**gang**	贡 – 貢
费 – 費	绋 – 紼	冈 – 岡	唝 – 嗊
镄 – 鐨	辅 – 輔	刚 – 剛	**gou**
fen	抚 – 撫	枫 – 棡	缑 – 緱
纷 – 紛	赋 – 賦	纲 – 綱	沟 – 溝
坟 – 墳	赙 – 賻	钢 – 鋼	钩 – 鉤
豮 – 豶	缚 – 縛	㧏 – 掆	觏 – 覯
粪 – 糞	讣 – 訃	岗 – 崗	诟 – 詬
愤 – 憤	复 – 復	**gao**	构 – 構
偾 – 僨	複	镐 – 鎬	购 – 購
奋 – 奮	覆	缟 – 縞	**gu**
feng	鳆 – 鰒	诰 – 誥	轱 – 軲
丰 – 豐	驸 – 駙	锆 – 鋯	鸪 – 鴣
沣 – 灃	鲋 – 鮒	**ge**	诂 – 詁
锋 – 鋒	负 – 負	鸽 – 鴿	钴 – 鈷
风 – 風	妇 – 婦	搁 – 擱	贾 – 賈
沨 – 渢	**G**	镉 – 鎘	蛊 – 蠱
疯 – 瘋	**ga**	颌 – 頜	毂 – 轂
枫 – 楓	钆 – 釓	阁 – 閣	馉 – 餶
砜 – 碸	**gai**	个 – 個	鹘 – 鶻
冯 – 馮	该 – 該	铬 – 鉻	谷 – 穀
缝 – 縫	赅 – 賅	**gei**	鹄 – 鵠
讽 – 諷	盖 – 蓋	给 – 給	顾 – 顧
凤 – 鳳	钙 – 鈣	**geng**	锢 – 錮
赗 – 賵	**gan**	赓 – 賡	**gua**
fu	干 – 乾	鹒 – 鶊	刮 – 颳
麸 – 麩	幹	鲠 – 鯁	鸹 – 鴰
肤 – 膚	尴 – 尷	绠 – 綆	剐 – 剮

诖 – 詿

guan

关 – 關
纶 – 綸
鳏 – 鰥
观 – 觀
馆 – 館
鹳 – 鸛
贯 – 貫
惯 – 慣
掼 – 摜

guang

广 – 廣
犷 – 獷

gui

妫 – 嬀
沩 – 溈
规 – 規
鲑 – 鮭
闺 – 閨
归 – 歸
龟 – 龜
轨 – 軌
匦 – 匭
诡 – 詭
鳜 – 鱖
柜 – 櫃
贵 – 貴
刿 – 劌
桧 – 檜
刽 – 劊

gun

辊 – 輥
绲 – 緄
鲧 – 鯀

guo

涡 – 渦
埚 – 堝
锅 – 鍋
蝈 – 蟈
国 – 國
掴 – 摑
帼 – 幗
馃 – 餜
腘 – 膕
过 – 過

H

ha

铪 – 鉿

hai

还 – 還
骇 – 駭

han

顸 – 頇
韩 – 韓
阚 – 闞
喊 – 喊
汉 – 漢
颔 – 頷

hang

绗 – 絎
颃 – 頏

hao

颢 – 顥
灏 – 灝
号 – 號

he

诃 – 訶
阂 – 閡
阖 – 闔
鹖 – 鶡
颌 – 頜
饸 – 餄
合 – 閤
纥 – 紇
鹤 – 鶴
贺 – 賀
吓 – 嚇

heng

鸻 – 鴴

hong

轰 – 轟
黉 – 黌
鸿 – 鴻
红 – 紅
荭 – 葒
讧 – 訌

hou

后 – 後
鲎 – 鱟

hu

轷 – 軤
壶 – 壺

胡 – 鬍
鹕 – 鶘
鹄 – 鵠
鹘 – 鶻
浒 – 滸
沪 – 滬
护 – 護

hua

华 – 華
骅 – 驊
哗 – 嘩
铧 – 鏵
画 – 畫
婳 – 嫿
划 – 劃
桦 – 樺
话 – 話

huai

怀 – 懷
坏 – 壞

huan

欢 – 歡
还 – 還
环 – 環
缳 – 繯
镮 – 鐶
缓 – 緩
鲩 – 鯇

huang

鳇 – 鰉
谎 – 謊

hui	货 – 貨	绩 – 績	坚 – 堅
挥 – 揮	**J**	计 – 計	鲣 – 鰹
辉 – 輝	**ji**	系 – 繫	缄 – 緘
翚 – 翬	赍 – 齎	骥 – 驥	鞯 – 韉
诙 – 詼	跻 – 躋	觊 – 覬	监 – 監
回 – 迴	击 – 擊	蓟 – 薊	歼 – 殲
汇 – 匯	赍 – 賫	鲫 – 鯽	艰 – 艱
彙	缉 – 緝	记 – 記	间 – 間
贿 – 賄	积 – 積	纪 – 紀	谫 – 謭
秽 – 穢	羁 – 羈	继 – 繼	硷 – 礆
会 – 會	机 – 機	**jia**	拣 – 揀
烩 – 燴	饥 – 饑	家 – 傢	笕 – 筧
荟 – 薈	讥 – 譏	镓 – 鎵	茧 – 繭
绘 – 繪	玑 – 璣	夹 – 夾	检 – 檢
诲 – 誨	矶 – 磯	浃 – 浹	捡 – 撿
殨 – 殨	叽 – 嘰	颊 – 頰	睑 – 瞼
讳 – 諱	鸡 – 雞	荚 – 莢	俭 – 儉
hun	鹡 – 鶺	蛱 – 蛺	裥 – 襇
荤 – 葷	辑 – 輯	铗 – 鋏	简 – 簡
阍 – 閽	极 – 極	郏 – 郟	谏 – 諫
浑 – 渾	级 – 級	贾 – 賈	渐 – 漸
珲 – 琿	挤 – 擠	槚 – 檟	槛 – 檻
馄 – 餛	给 – 給	钾 – 鉀	贱 – 賤
诨 – 諢	几 – 幾	价 – 價	溅 – 濺
huo	虮 – 蟣	驾 – 駕	践 – 踐
钬 – 鈥	济 – 濟	**jian**	钱 – 錢
伙 – 夥	霁 – 霽	鹣 – 鶼	荐 – 薦
镬 – 鑊	荠 – 薺	鳒 – 鰜	鉴 – 鑒
获 – 獲	剂 – 劑	缣 – 縑	见 – 見
穫	鲚 – 鱭	戋 – 戔	枧 – 梘
祸 – 禍	际 – 際	笺 – 箋	舰 – 艦

剑 – 劍	较 – 較	荩 – 藎	龃 – 齟
键 – 鍵	轿 – 轎	赆 – 贐	榉 – 櫸
涧 – 澗	挢 – 撟	烬 – 燼	讵 – 詎
铜 – 鐧	峤 – 嶠	**jing**	惧 – 懼
jiang	**jie**	惊 – 驚	飓 – 颶
姜 – 薑	阶 – 階	鲸 – 鯨	窭 – 窶
将 – 將	疖 – 癤	鹊 – 鵲	屦 – 屨
浆 – 漿	讦 – 訐	泾 – 涇	据 – 據
缰 – 繮	洁 – 潔	茎 – 莖	剧 – 劇
讲 – 講	诘 – 詰	经 – 經	锯 – 鋸
桨 – 槳	撷 – 擷	颈 – 頸	**juan**
奖 – 獎	颉 – 頡	刭 – 剄	鹃 – 鵑
蒋 – 蔣	结 – 結	镜 – 鏡	镌 – 鐫
酱 – 醬	鲒 – 鮚	竞 – 競	卷 – 捲
绛 – 絳	节 – 節	痉 – 痙	绢 – 絹
jiao	借 – 籍	劲 – 勁	**jue**
胶 – 膠	诫 – 誡	胫 – 脛	觉 – 覺
鲛 – 鮫	**jin**	径 – 徑	镢 – 钁
鹪 – 鷦	谨 – 謹	靓 – 靚	镢 – 钁
浇 – 澆	馑 – 饉	**jiu**	谲 – 譎
骄 – 驕	觐 – 覲	纠 – 糾	诀 – 訣
娇 – 嬌	紧 – 緊	鸠 – 鳩	绝 – 絕
鹪 – 鷦	锦 – 錦	阄 – 鬮	**jun**
饺 – 餃	仅 – 僅	鹫 – 鷲	军 – 軍
铰 – 鉸	劲 – 勁	旧 – 舊	鞍 – 鞿
绞 – 絞	进 – 進	**ju**	钧 – 鈞
侥 – 僥	琎 – 璡	车 – 車	骏 – 駿
矫 – 矯	缙 – 縉	驹 – 駒	**K**
搅 – 攪	尽 – 盡	鶋 – 鶋	**kai**
缴 – 繳	– 儘	锔 – 鋦	开 – 開
觉 – 覺	浕 – 濜	举 – 舉	锎 – 鐦

恺 – 愷	**kou**	邝 – 鄺	莱 – 萊
垲 – 塏	抠 – 摳	赈 – 覼	崃 – 崍
剀 – 剴	眍 – 瞘	**kui**	铼 – 錸
铠 – 鎧	**ku**	窥 – 窺	徕 – 徠
凯 – 凱	库 – 庫	亏 – 虧	赖 – 賴
阊 – 闓	裤 – 褲	岿 – 巋	濑 – 瀨
锴 – 鍇	绔 – 絝	溃 – 潰	癞 – 癩
忾 – 愾	喾 – 嚳	禈 – 禩	籁 – 籟
kan	**kua**	愦 – 憒	睐 – 睞
龛 – 龕	夸 – 誇	聩 – 聵	赉 – 賚
槛 – 檻	**kuai**	匮 – 匱	**lan**
kang	扣 – 擓	蒉 – 蕢	兰 – 蘭
钪 – 鈧	会 – 會	馈 – 饋	栏 – 欄
kao	浍 – 澮	篑 – 簣	拦 – 攔
铐 – 銬	哙 – 噲	**kun**	阑 – 闌
ke	郐 – 鄶	鲲 – 鯤	澜 – 瀾
颏 – 頦	侩 – 儈	锟 – 錕	谰 – 讕
轲 – 軻	脍 – 膾	壸 – 壼	斓 – 斕
钶 – 鈳	鲙 – 鱠	阃 – 閫	镧 – 鑭
颗 – 顆	狯 – 獪	困 – 睏	褴 – 襤
壳 – 殼	块 – 塊	**kuo**	蓝 – 藍
缂 – 緙	**kuan**	阔 – 闊	篮 – 籃
克 – 剋	宽 – 寬	扩 – 擴	岚 – 嵐
课 – 課	髋 – 髖	**L**	懒 – 懶
骒 – 騍	**kuang**	**la**	览 – 覽
锞 – 錁	诓 – 誆	蜡 – 蠟	榄 – 欖
ken	诳 – 誑	腊 – 臘	揽 – 攬
恳 – 懇	矿 – 礦	镴 – 鑞	缆 – 纜
垦 – 墾	圹 – 壙	**lai**	烂 – 爛
keng	旷 – 曠	来 – 來	滥 – 濫
铿 – 鏗	纩 – 纊	涞 – 淶	**lang**

银 – 銀	礼 – 禮	帘 – 簾	缭 – 繚
阆 – 閬	逦 – 邐	镰 – 鐮	疗 – 療
lao	里 – 裏	联 – 聯	辽 – 遼
捞 – 撈	锂 – 鋰	连 – 連	了 – 瞭
劳 – 勞	鲤 – 鯉	涟 – 漣	钌 – 釕
崂 – 嶗	鳢 – 鱧	莲 – 蓮	镣 – 鐐
痨 – 癆	丽 – 麗	鲢 – 鰱	**lie**
铹 – 鐒	俪 – 儷	琏 – 璉	猎 – 獵
铑 – 銠	郦 – 酈	奁 – 奩	鸷 – 鴷
涝 – 澇	厉 – 厲	怜 – 憐	**lin**
唠 – 嘮	励 – 勵	敛 – 斂	辚 – 轔
耢 – 耮	砺 – 礪	蔹 – 蘞	鳞 – 鱗
le	历 – 歷	脸 – 臉	临 – 臨
鳓 – 鰳	厤 – 曆	恋 – 戀	邻 – 鄰
乐 – 樂	沥 – 瀝	链 – 鏈	蔺 – 藺
饹 – 餎	坜 – 壢	炼 – 煉	躏 – 躪
lei	疬 – 癧	练 – 練	赁 – 賃
镭 – 鐳	雳 – 靂	潋 – 瀲	**ling**
累 – 纍	枥 – 櫪	殓 – 殮	鲮 – 鯪
缧 – 縲	苈 – 藶	裣 – 襝	绫 – 綾
诔 – 誄	呖 – 嚦	裢 – 褳	龄 – 齡
垒 – 壘	疠 – 癘	**liang**	铃 – 鈴
类 – 類	粝 – 糲	粮 – 糧	鸰 – 鴒
li	砾 – 礫	两 – 兩	灵 – 靈
离 – 離	蛎 – 蠣	俩 – 倆	棂 – 欞
漓 – 灕	栎 – 櫟	啢 – 啢	领 – 領
篱 – 籬	轹 – 轢	魉 – 魎	岭 – 嶺
缡 – 縭	隶 – 隸	谅 – 諒	**liu**
骊 – 驪	**lia**	辆 – 輛	飑 – 飀
鹂 – 鸝	俩 – 倆	**liao**	刘 – 劉
鲡 – 鱺	**lian**	鹩 – 鷯	浏 – 瀏

骝 – 騮	楼 – 樓	陆 – 陸	仑 – 侖
镏 – 鎦	搂 – 摟	录 – 録	沦 – 淪
绺 – 綹	嵝 – 嶁	箓 – 籙	轮 – 輪
馏 – 餾	篓 – 簍	绿 – 綠	囵 – 圇
鹨 – 鷚	瘘 – 瘻	铲 – 轤	纶 – 綸
陆 – 陸	镂 – 鏤	氆 – 氌	伦 – 倫
long	**lu**	**lü**	论 – 論
龙 – 龍	噜 – 嚕	驴 – 驢	**luo**
泷 – 瀧	庐 – 廬	闾 – 閭	骡 – 騾
珑 – 瓏	炉 – 爐	榈 – 櫚	脶 – 腡
聋 – 聾	芦 – 蘆	屡 – 屢	罗 – 羅
栊 – 櫳	卢 – 盧	偻 – 僂	囉
砻 – 礱	泸 – 瀘	褛 – 褸	逻 – 邏
笼 – 籠	垆 – 壚	缕 – 縷	萝 – 蘿
茏 – 蘢	栌 – 櫨	铝 – 鋁	锣 – 鑼
咙 – 嚨	颅 – 顱	虑 – 慮	箩 – 籮
昽 – 曨	鸬 – 鸕	滤 – 濾	椤 – 欏
胧 – 朧	胪 – 臚	绿 – 綠	猡 – 玀
垄 – 壟	鲈 – 鱸	**luan**	荦 – 犖
拢 – 攏	舻 – 艫	娈 – 孌	泺 – 濼
陇 – 隴	卤 – 鹵	栾 – 欒	骆 – 駱
lou	滷	滦 – 灤	络 – 絡
睽 – 瞜	虏 – 虜	峦 – 巒	**M**
娄 – 婁	掳 – 擄	脔 – 臠	**m**
偻 – 僂	鲁 – 魯	銮 – 鑾	呒 – 嘸
喽 – 嘍	橹 – 櫓	挛 – 攣	**ma**
楼 – 樓	镥 – 鑥	孪 – 孿	妈 – 媽
溇 – 漊	辘 – 轆	乱 – 亂	马 – 馬
蒌 – 蔞	轳 – 轤	**lun**	蚂 – 螞
髅 – 髏	赂 – 賂	抡 – 掄	玛 – 瑪
蝼 – 螻	鹭 – 鷺		码 – 碼

犸 – 獁
骂 – 罵
吗 – 嗎
唛 – 嘜

mai

买 – 買
麦 – 麥
卖 – 賣
迈 – 邁
荬 – 蕒

man

颟 – 顢
馒 – 饅
鳗 – 鰻
蛮 – 蠻
瞒 – 瞞
满 – 滿
螨 – 蟎
谩 – 謾
缦 – 縵
镘 – 鏝

mang

铓 – 鋩

mao

锚 – 錨
铆 – 鉚
贸 – 貿

me

么 – 麼

mei

霉 – 黴

锯 – 鋸
鹛 – 鶥
镁 – 鎂

men

门 – 門
扪 – 捫
钔 – 鍆
懑 – 懣
闷 – 悶
焖 – 燜
们 – 們

meng

蒙 – 矇
　　 – 濛
　　 – 懞
锰 – 錳
梦 – 夢

mi

谜 – 謎
祢 – 禰
弥 – 彌
　　 – 瀰
猕 – 獼
谧 – 謐
觅 – 覓

mian

绵 – 綿
渑 – 澠
缅 – 緬
面 – 麵

miao

鹋 – 鶓
缈 – 緲
缪 – 繆
庙 – 廟

mie

灭 – 滅
蔑 – 衊

min

缗 – 緡
闵 – 閔
悯 – 憫
闽 – 閩
黾 – 黽
鳘 – 鰵

ming

鸣 – 鳴
铭 – 銘

miu

谬 – 謬
缪 – 繆

mo

谟 – 謨
馍 – 饃
蓦 – 驀

mou

谋 – 謀
缪 – 繆

mu

亩 – 畝
钼 – 鉬

N

na

镎 – 鎿
钠 – 鈉
纳 – 納

nan

难 – 難

nang

馕 – 饢

nao

挠 – 撓
蛲 – 蟯
铙 – 鐃
恼 – 惱
脑 – 腦
闹 – 鬧

ne

讷 – 訥

nei

馁 – 餒

ni

鲵 – 鯢
铌 – 鈮
拟 – 擬
腻 – 膩

nian

鲇 – 鮎
鲶 – 鯰
辇 – 輦
撵 – 攆

niang	nu	孿 – 孿	钋 – 釙
酿 – 釀	驽 – 駑	**pen**	颇 – 頗
niao	**nü**	喷 – 噴	泼 – 潑
鸟 – 鳥	钕 – 釹	**peng**	钹 – 鏺
茑 – 蔦	**nüe**	鹏 – 鵬	钷 – 鉕
袅 – 裊	疟 – 瘧	**pi**	**pu**
nie	**nuo**	纰 – 紕	铺 – 鋪
聂 – 聶	傩 – 儺	罴 – 羆	扑 – 撲
颞 – 顳	诺 – 諾	鲏 – 鮍	仆 – 僕
嗫 – 囁	锘 – 鍩	铍 – 鈹	镤 – 鏷
蹑 – 躡	**O**	辟 – 闢	谱 – 譜
镊 – 鑷	**ou**	鹏 – 鸊	镨 – 鐠
啮 – 嚙	区 – 區	**pian**	朴 – 樸
镍 – 鎳	讴 – 謳	骈 – 駢	**Q**
ning	瓯 – 甌	谝 – 諞	**qi**
宁 – 寧	鸥 – 鷗	骗 – 騙	缉 – 緝
柠 – 檸	殴 – 毆	**piao**	桤 – 榿
咛 – 嚀	欧 – 歐	飘 – 飄	齐 – 齊
狞 – 獰	呕 – 嘔	缥 – 縹	蛴 – 蠐
聍 – 聹	沤 – 漚	骠 – 驃	脐 – 臍
拧 – 擰	怄 – 慪	**pin**	骑 – 騎
泞 – 濘	**P**	嫔 – 嬪	骐 – 騏
niu	**pan**	频 – 頻	鳍 – 鰭
钮 – 鈕	蹒 – 蹣	颦 – 顰	颀 – 頎
纽 – 紐	盘 – 盤	贫 – 貧	蕲 – 蘄
nong	**pang**	**ping**	启 – 啓
农 – 農	鳑 – 鰟	评 – 評	绮 – 綺
浓 – 濃	庞 – 龐	苹 – 蘋	岂 – 豈
侬 – 儂	**pei**	鲆 – 鮃	碛 – 磧
脓 – 膿	赔 – 賠	凭 – 憑	气 – 氣
哝 – 噥	锫 – 錇	**po**	讫 – 訖

荞 – 蕎

qian

骞 – 騫
谦 – 謙
悭 – 慳
牵 – 牽
佥 – 僉
签 – 簽
　 – 籤
千 – 韆
迁 – 遷
钎 – 釺
铅 – 鉛
鸽 – 鵮
荨 – 蕁
钳 – 鉗
钱 – 錢
钤 – 鈐
浅 – 淺
遣 – 譴
缱 – 繾
堑 – 塹
椠 – 槧
纤 – 縴

qiang

玱 – 瑲
枪 – 槍
锖 – 錆
墙 – 墻
蔷 – 薔
樯 – 檣

嫱 – 嬙
锵 – 鏘
羟 – 羥
抢 – 搶
炝 – 熗
饯 – 餸
跄 – 蹌
呛 – 嗆

qiao

硗 – 磽
跷 – 蹺
锹 – 鍬
缲 – 繰
翘 – 翹
乔 – 喬
桥 – 橋
硚 – 礄
侨 – 僑
鞒 – 鞽
荞 – 蕎
谯 – 譙
壳 – 殼
窍 – 竅
诮 – 誚

qie

锲 – 鍥
惬 – 愜
箧 – 篋
窃 – 竊

qin

亲 – 親

钦 – 欽
嵚 – 嶔
骎 – 駸
寝 – 寢
锓 – 鋟
揿 – 撳

qing

鲭 – 鯖
轻 – 輕
氢 – 氫
倾 – 傾
䝼 – 䝼
请 – 請
顷 – 頃
庼 – 廎
庆 – 慶

qiong

穷 – 窮
劳 – 藭
琼 – 瓊
茕 – 煢

qiu

秋 – 鞦
鸺 – 鵂
鳅 – 鰍
鳈 – 鰁
巯 – 巰

qu

曲 – 麴
区 – 區
驱 – 驅

岖 – 嶇
躯 – 軀
诎 – 詘
趋 – 趨
鸲 – 鴝
龋 – 齲
觑 – 覷
阒 – 闃

quan

权 – 權
颧 – 顴
铨 – 銓
诠 – 詮
绻 – 綣
劝 – 勸

que

悫 – 愨
鹊 – 鵲
阙 – 闕
确 – 確
阕 – 闋

R

rang

让 – 讓

rao

桡 – 橈
荛 – 蕘
饶 – 饒
娆 – 嬈
扰 – 擾
绕 – 繞

re

热 – 熱

ren

认 – 認

饪 – 飪

纴 – 紝

韧 – 靭

纫 – 紉

韧 – 韌

rong

荣 – 榮

蝾 – 蠑

嵘 – 嶸

绒 – 絨

ru

铷 – 銣

颥 – 顬

缛 – 縟

ruan

软 – 軟

rui

锐 – 銳

run

闰 – 閏

润 – 潤

S

sa

洒 – 灑

飒 – 颯

萨 – 薩

sai

鳃 – 鰓

赛 – 賽

san

毵 – 毿

馓 – 饊

伞 – 傘

sang

丧 – 喪

颡 – 顙

sao

骚 – 騷

缫 – 繅

扫 – 掃

se

涩 – 澀

啬 – 嗇

穑 – 穡

铯 – 銫

sha

鲨 – 鯊

纱 – 紗

杀 – 殺

铩 – 鎩

shai

筛 – 篩

晒 – 曬

shan

钐 – 釤

陕 – 陝

闪 – 閃

镨 – 鐥

鳝 – 鱔

缮 – 繕

掸 – 撣

骟 – 騸

镐 – 鐥

禅 – 禪

讪 – 訕

赡 – 贍

shang

殇 – 殤

觞 – 觴

伤 – 傷

赏 – 賞

shao

烧 – 燒

绍 – 紹

she

赊 – 賒

舍 – 捨

设 – 設

滠 – 灄

慑 – 懾

摄 – 攝

厍 – 厙

shei

谁 – 誰

shen

绅 – 紳

参 – 參

糁 – 糝

审 – 審

讅 – 讅

婶 – 嬸

沈 – 瀋

谂 – 諗

肾 – 腎

渗 – 滲

瘆 – 瘆

sheng

声 – 聲

渑 – 澠

绳 – 繩

胜 – 勝

圣 – 聖

shi

湿 – 濕

诗 – 詩

师 – 師

浉 – 溮

狮 – 獅

鸤 – 鳲

实 – 實

埘 – 塒

鲥 – 鰣

识 – 識

时 – 時

蚀 – 蝕

驶 – 駛

铈 – 鈰

视 – 視

谥 – 謚

试 – 試

轼 – 軾
势 – 勢
莳 – 蒔
贳 – 貰
释 – 釋
饰 – 飾
适 – 適

shou

兽 – 獸
寿 – 壽
绶 – 綬

shu

枢 – 樞
摅 – 攄
输 – 輸
纾 – 紓
书 – 書
赎 – 贖
属 – 屬
数 – 數
树 – 樹
术 – 術
竖 – 豎

shuai

帅 – 帥

shuan

闩 – 閂

shuang

双 – 雙
泷 – 瀧

shui

谁 – 誰

shun

顺 – 順

shuo

说 – 說
硕 – 碩
烁 – 爍
铄 – 鑠

si

锶 – 鍶
飔 – 颸
酾 – 釃
缌 – 緦
丝 – 絲
咝 – 噝
鸶 – 鷥
蛳 – 螄
驷 – 駟
饲 – 飼

song

松 – 鬆
怂 – 慫
耸 – 聳
扨 – 摟
讼 – 訟
颂 – 頌
诵 – 誦

sou

馊 – 餿
锼 – 鎪
飕 – 颼

薮 – 藪
擞 – 擻

su

苏 – 蘇
　　囌
稣 – 穌
谡 – 謖
诉 – 訴
肃 – 肅

sui

虽 – 雖
随 – 隨
绥 – 綏
岁 – 歲
谇 – 誶

sun

孙 – 孫
荪 – 蓀
狲 – 猻
损 – 損

suo

缩 – 縮
琐 – 瑣
唢 – 嗩
锁 – 鎖

T

ta

铊 – 鉈
鳎 – 鰨
獭 – 獺
汰 – 澾

挞 – 撻
闼 – 闥

tai

台 – 臺
　　檯
　　颱
骀 – 駘
鲐 – 鮐
态 – 態
钛 – 鈦

tan

滩 – 灘
瘫 – 癱
摊 – 攤
贪 – 貪
谈 – 談
坛 – 壇
　　罎
谭 – 譚
昙 – 曇
弹 – 彈
钽 – 鉭
叹 – 嘆

tang

镗 – 鏜
汤 – 湯
傥 – 儻
锐 – 钂
烫 – 燙

tao

涛 – 濤

韬 – 韜
绦 – 縧
焘 – 燾
讨 – 討

te

铽 – 鋱

teng

誊 – 謄
腾 – 騰
滕 – 縢

ti

锑 – 銻
鹈 – 鵜
绨 – 綈
缇 – 緹
题 – 題
体 – 體

tian

阗 – 闐

tiao

条 – 條
鲦 – 鰷
髫 – 鰼
调 – 調
粜 – 糶

tie

贴 – 貼
铁 – 鐵

ting

厅 – 廳

烃 – 烴
听 – 聽
颋 – 頲
铤 – 鋌

tong

铜 – 銅
鲖 – 鮦
统 – 統
恸 – 慟

tou

头 – 頭

tu

图 – 圖
涂 – 塗
钍 – 釷

tuan

抟 – 摶
团 – 團
糰

tui

颓 – 頹

tun

饨 – 飩

tuo

饦 – 飥
驼 – 駝
鸵 – 鴕
驮 – 馱
鼍 – 鼉
椭 – 橢
萚 – 蘀

箨 – 籜

W

wa

娲 – 媧
洼 – 窪
袜 – 襪

wai

呙 – 喎

wan

弯 – 彎
湾 – 灣
纨 – 紈
顽 – 頑
绾 – 綰
万 – 萬

wang

网 – 網
辋 – 輞

wei

为 – 爲
维 – 維
潍 – 濰
韦 – 韋
违 – 違
围 – 圍
涠 – 潿
帏 – 幃
闱 – 闈
伪 – 僞
鲔 – 鮪
诿 – 諉

炜 – 煒
玮 – 瑋
苇 – 葦
韪 – 韙
伟 – 偉
纬 – 緯
砘 – 磈
谓 – 謂
卫 – 衛

wen

鳁 – 鰛
纹 – 紋
闻 – 聞
阌 – 閿
稳 – 穩
问 – 問

wo

涡 – 渦
窝 – 窩
莴 – 萵
蜗 – 蝸
挝 – 撾
龌 – 齷

wu

诬 – 誣
乌 – 烏
呜 – 嗚
钨 – 鎢
邬 – 鄔
无 – 無
芜 – 蕪

妩 – 嫵	峡 – 峽	馅 – 餡	撷 – 擷
怃 – 憮	侠 – 俠	**xiang**	缬 – 纈
庑 – 廡	狭 – 狹	骧 – 驤	协 – 協
鹉 – 鵡	吓 – 嚇	镶 – 鑲	挟 – 挾
坞 – 塢	**xian**	乡 – 鄉	胁 – 脅
务 – 務	鲜 – 鮮	芗 – 薌	谐 – 諧
雾 – 霧	纤 – 纖	缃 – 緗	亵 – 褻
骛 – 騖	跹 – 躚	详 – 詳	泻 – 瀉
鹜 – 鶩	锨 – 鍁	鲞 – 鯗	绁 – 紲
误 – 誤	莶 – 薟	响 – 響	谢 – 謝
X	贤 – 賢	饷 – 餉	**xin**
xi	咸 – 鹹	飨 – 饗	锌 – 鋅
牺 – 犧	衔 – 銜	向 – 嚮	䜣 – 訢
饻 – 餏	挦 – 撏	象 – 像	衅 – 釁
锡 – 錫	闲 – 閑	项 – 項	**xing**
袭 – 襲	鹇 – 鷴	**xiao**	兴 – 興
觋 – 覡	娴 – 嫻	骁 – 驍	荥 – 滎
习 – 習	痫 – 癇	哓 – 嘵	钘 – 鈃
鳛 – 鰼	藓 – 蘚	销 – 銷	铏 – 鉶
玺 – 璽	蚬 – 蜆	绡 – 綃	陉 – 陘
铣 – 銑	显 – 顯	嚣 – 囂	饧 – 餳
系 – 係	险 – 險	枭 – 梟	**xiong**
繫	猃 – 獫	鸮 – 鴞	讻 – 訩
细 – 細	铣 – 銑	萧 – 蕭	诇 – 詗
阋 – 鬩	献 – 獻	潇 – 瀟	**xiu**
戏 – 戲	线 – 綫	蟏 – 蠨	馐 – 饈
饩 – 餼	现 – 現	箫 – 簫	鸺 – 鵂
xia	苋 – 莧	晓 – 曉	绣 – 綉
虾 – 蝦	岘 – 峴	啸 – 嘯	锈 – 銹
辖 – 轄	县 – 縣	**xie**	**xu**
硖 – 硤	宪 – 憲	颉 – 頡	

驿 – 驛	嘤 – 嚶	邮 – 郵	渊 – 渂
峄 – 嶧	鹦 – 鸚	铕 – 銪	薗 – 蕒
绎 – 繹	缨 – 纓	诱 – 誘	鹓 – 鵷
义 – 義	荧 – 熒	**yu**	**yuan**
议 – 議	莹 – 瑩	纡 – 紆	渊 – 淵
轶 – 軼	茔 – 塋	舆 – 輿	鸢 – 鳶
艺 – 藝	萤 – 螢	欤 – 歟	鸳 – 鴛
呓 – 囈	萦 – 縈	余 – 餘	鼋 – 黿
亿 – 億	营 – 營	觎 – 覦	园 – 園
忆 – 憶	赢 – 贏	谀 – 諛	辕 – 轅
诣 – 詣	蝇 – 蠅	鱼 – 魚	员 – 員
镱 – 鐿	瘿 – 癭	渔 – 漁	圆 – 圓
yin	颖 – 穎	歔 – 歔	缘 – 緣
铟 – 銦	颍 – 潁	与 – 與	橼 – 櫞
阴 – 陰	**yo**	语 – 語	远 – 遠
荫 – 蔭	哟 – 喲	龉 – 齬	愿 – 願
龈 – 齦	**yong**	伛 – 傴	**yue**
银 – 銀	痈 – 癰	屿 – 嶼	约 – 約
饮 – 飲	拥 – 擁	誉 – 譽	哕 – 噦
隐 – 隱	佣 – 傭	钰 – 鈺	阅 – 閱
瘾 – 癮	镛 – 鏞	吁 – 籲	钺 – 鉞
卿 – 卿	鳙 – 鱅	御 – 禦	跃 – 躍
ying	颙 – 顒	驭 – 馭	乐 – 樂
应 – 應	踊 – 踴	阈 – 閾	钥 – 鑰
鹰 – 鷹	**you**	妪 – 嫗	**yun**
莺 – 鶯	忧 – 憂	郁 – 鬱	云 – 雲
罂 – 罌	优 – 優	谕 – 諭	芸 – 蕓
婴 – 嬰	鱿 – 魷	鹆 – 鵒	纭 – 紜
璎 – 瓔	犹 – 猶	饫 – 飫	陨 – 隕
樱 – 櫻	莸 – 蕕	狱 – 獄	郧 – 鄖
撄 – 攖	铀 – 鈾	预 – 預	殒 – 殞

陨 – 隕	**ze**	毡 – 氈	鹧 – 鷓
恽 – 惲	责 – 責	觇 – 覘	**zhen**
晕 – 暈	赜 – 賾	谵 – 譫	针 – 針
郓 – 鄆	喷 – 嘖	斩 – 斬	贞 – 貞
运 – 運	帻 – 幘	崭 – 嶄	浈 – 湞
酝 – 醞	箦 – 簀	盏 – 盞	祯 – 禎
韫 – 韞	则 – 則	辗 – 輾	桢 – 楨
缊 – 縕	铡 – 鍘	绽 – 綻	侦 – 偵
蕴 – 蘊	泽 – 澤	颤 – 顫	缜 – 縝
Z	择 – 擇	栈 – 棧	诊 – 診
za	**zei**	战 – 戰	轸 – 軫
臜 – 臢	贼 – 賊	**zhang**	鸩 – 鴆
杂 – 雜	**zen**	张 – 張	赈 – 賑
zai	谮 – 譖	长 – 長	镇 – 鎮
载 – 載	**zeng**	涨 – 漲	纼 – 紖
zan	缯 – 繒	帐 – 帳	阵 – 陣
趱 – 趲	赠 – 贈	账 – 賬	**zheng**
攒 – 攢	锃 – 鋥	胀 – 脹	钲 – 鉦
錾 – 鏨	**zha**	**zhao**	征 – 徵
暂 – 暫	铡 – 鍘	钊 – 釗	铮 – 錚
赞 – 贊	闸 – 閘	赵 – 趙	症 – 癥
瓒 – 瓚	轧 – 軋	诏 – 詔	郑 – 鄭
zang	羞 – 羞	**zhe**	证 – 證
赃 – 臟	鲊 – 鮓	谪 – 謫	帧 – 幀
脏 – 臟	诈 – 詐	辙 – 轍	诤 – 諍
髒	**zhai**	蛰 – 蟄	阐 – 闡
驵 – 駔	斋 – 齋	辄 – 輒	**zhi**
zao	债 – 債	謺 – 讋	只 – 隻
凿 – 鑿	**zhan**	折 – 摺	祇
枣 – 棗	鹯 – 鸇	锗 – 鍺	织 – 織
灶 – 竈	鳣 – 鱣	这 – 這	职 – 職

蹰 – 躕	纠 – 紏	赚 – 賺	龇 – 齜
执 – 執	刍 – 芻	传 – 傳	辎 – 輜
萦 – 縈	骤 – 驟	馔 – 饌	锱 – 錙
纸 – 紙	皱 – 皺	**zhuang**	缁 – 緇
挚 – 摯	绉 – 縐	妆 – 妝	鲻 – 鯔
贽 – 贄	㤘 – 㤘	装 – 裝	渍 – 漬
鸷 – 鷙	㑇 – 㑇	庄 – 莊	**zong**
掷 – 擲	昼 – 晝	桩 – 樁	综 – 綜
滞 – 滯	**zhu**	戆 – 戇	枞 – 樅
栉 – 櫛	诸 – 諸	壮 – 壯	总 – 總
轾 – 輊	槠 – 櫧	状 – 狀	纵 – 縱
致 – 緻	朱 – 硃	**zhui**	**zou**
帜 – 幟	诛 – 誅	骓 – 騅	诹 – 諏
制 – 製	铢 – 銖	锥 – 錐	鲰 – 鯫
质 – 質	烛 – 燭	赘 – 贅	驺 – 騶
踬 – 躓	嘱 – 囑	缒 – 縋	邹 – 鄒
锧 – 鑕	瞩 – 矚	缀 – 綴	**zu**
骘 – 騭	贮 – 貯	坠 – 墜	镞 – 鏃
zhong	驻 – 駐	**zhun**	诅 – 詛
终 – 終	铸 – 鑄	谆 – 諄	组 – 組
钟 – 鐘	筑 – 築	准 – 準	**zuan**
鍾	**zhua**	**zhuo**	钻 – 鑽
种 – 種	挝 – 撾	锗 – 鐯	躜 – 躦
肿 – 腫	**zhuan**	浊 – 濁	缵 – 纘
众 – 眾	专 – 專	诼 – 諑	赚 – 賺
zhou	砖 – 磚	镯 – 鐲	**zun**
诌 – 謅	䏝 – 膞	**zi**	鳟 – 鱒
赒 – 賙	颛 – 顓	谘 – 諮	**zuo**
鸼 – 鵃	转 – 轉	资 – 資	凿 – 鑿
轴 – 軸	啭 – 囀	镃 – 鎡	

Strokes Index
笔画索引

帅 – 帥
归 – 歸
叶 – 葉
号 – 號
电 – 電
只 – 隻
– 祇
叽 – 嘰
叹 – 嘆

【丿】

们 – 們
仪 – 儀
丛 – 叢
尔 – 爾
乐 – 樂
处 – 處
冬 – 鼕
鸟 – 鳥
务 – 務
刍 – 芻
饥 – 饑
– 飢

【丶】

邝 – 鄺
冯 – 馮
闪 – 閃
兰 – 蘭
汇 – 匯
– 彙
头 – 頭
汉 – 漢

宁 – 寧
它 – 牠
讦 – 訐
讧 – 訌
讨 – 討
写 – 寫
让 – 讓
礼 – 禮
讪 – 訕
讫 – 訖
训 – 訓
议 – 議
讯 – 訊
记 – 記

【一】

辽 – 遼
边 – 邊
出 – 齣
发 – 發
– 髮
圣 – 聖
对 – 對
台 – 臺
– 檯
– 颱
纠 – 糾
驭 – 馭
丝 – 絲

6画

【一】

玑 – 璣
动 – 動
执 – 執
巩 – 鞏
圹 – 壙
扩 – 擴
扪 – 捫
扫 – 掃
扬 – 揚
场 – 場
亚 – 亞
芗 – 薌
朴 – 樸
机 – 機
权 – 權
过 – 過
协 – 協
压 – 壓
厌 – 厭
库 – 庫
页 – 頁
夸 – 誇
夺 – 奪
达 – 達
夹 – 夾
轨 – 軌
尧 – 堯
划 – 劃
迈 – 邁
毕 – 畢

【丨】

贞 – 貞
师 – 師
当 – 當
– 噹
尘 – 塵
吁 – 籲
吓 – 嚇
虫 – 蟲
曲 – 麯
团 – 團
– 糰
吗 – 嗎
屿 – 嶼
岁 – 歲
回 – 迴
岂 – 豈
则 – 則
刚 – 剛
网 – 網

【丿】

钆 – 釓
钇 – 釔
朱 – 硃
迁 – 遷
乔 – 喬
伟 – 偉
传 – 傳
伛 – 傴
优 – 優
伤 – 傷
伥 – 倀

价 – 價	产 – 産	异 – 異	寿 – 壽
伦 – 倫	闭 – 閉	导 – 導	麦 – 麥
伧 – 傖	问 – 問	孙 – 孫	玛 – 瑪
华 – 華	闱 – 闈	阵 – 陣	进 – 進
伙 – 夥	关 – 關	阳 – 陽	远 – 遠
伪 – 僞	灯 – 燈	阶 – 階	违 – 違
向 – 嚮	汤 – 湯	阴 – 陰	韧 – 韌
后 – 後	忏 – 懺	妇 – 婦	划 – 劃
会 – 會	兴 – 興	妈 – 媽	运 – 運
杀 – 殺	讲 – 講	戏 – 戲	抚 – 撫
合 – 閤	讳 – 諱	观 – 觀	坛 – 壇
众 – 衆	讴 – 謳	欢 – 歡	– 罎
爷 – 爺	军 – 軍	买 – 買	抟 – 摶
伞 – 傘	讵 – 詎	纡 – 紆	坏 – 壞
创 – 創	讶 – 訝	红 – 紅	抠 – 摳
杂 – 雜	讷 – 訥	纠 – 糾	坜 – 壢
负 – 負	许 – 許	驮 – 馱	扰 – 擾
犷 – 獷	讹 – 訛	纤 – 縴	坝 – 壩
犸 – 獁	䜣 – 訢	– 纖	贡 – 貢
凫 – 鳬	论 – 論		抝 – 擰
邬 – 鄔	讻 – 訩	纥 – 紇	折 – 摺
饦 – 飥	讼 – 訟	驯 – 馴	抢 – 掄
饧 – 餳	讽 – 諷	纨 – 紈	抢 – 搶
【丶】	农 – 農	约 – 約	坞 – 塢
壮 – 壯	设 – 設	级 – 級	坟 – 墳
冲 – 衝	访 – 訪	纩 – 纊	护 – 護
妆 – 妝	诀 – 訣	纪 – 紀	壳 – 殼
庄 – 莊	【一】	驰 – 馳	块 – 塊
庆 – 慶	寻 – 尋	纫 – 紉	声 – 聲
刘 – 劉	尽 – 盡	**7 画**	报 – 報
齐 – 齊	– 儘	【一】	拟 – 擬

拟 – 擬	– 滷	岘 – 峴	饭 – 飯
芜 – 蕪	邺 – 鄴	帐 – 帳	饮 – 飲
苇 – 葦	坚 – 堅	岚 – 嵐	
芸 – 蕓	时 – 時	【 丿 】	系 – 係
苈 – 藶	呒 – 嘸	针 – 針	繫
苋 – 莧	县 – 縣	钉 – 釘	【 丶 】
苁 – 蓯	里 – 裏	钊 – 釗	冻 – 凍
苍 – 蒼	呓 – 囈	钋 – 釙	状 – 狀
严 – 嚴	呆 – 獃	钌 – 釕	亩 – 畝
芦 – 蘆	– 駄	乱 – 亂	庑 – 廡
劳 – 勞	呕 – 嘔	体 – 體	床 – 牀
克 – 剋	园 – 園	佣 – 傭	库 – 庫
苏 – 蘇	呖 – 嚦	伧 – 傖	疖 – 癤
– 囌	旷 – 曠	彻 – 徹	疗 – 療
极 – 極	围 – 圍	余 – 餘	应 – 應
杨 – 楊	吨 – 噸	佥 – 僉	这 – 這
两 – 兩	旸 – 暘	谷 – 穀	庐 – 廬
丽 – 麗	邮 – 郵	邻 – 鄰	弃 – 棄
医 – 醫	困 – 睏	肠 – 腸	闰 – 閏
励 – 勵	员 – 員	龟 – 龜	闱 – 闈
还 – 還	呗 – 唄	犹 – 猶	闲 – 閑
矶 – 磯	听 – 聽	狈 – 狽	间 – 間
奁 – 奩	呛 – 嗆	鸠 – 鳩	闵 – 閔
歼 – 殲	呜 – 嗚	条 – 條	闷 – 悶
来 – 來	别 – 彆	岛 – 島	灿 – 燦
欤 – 歟	财 – 財	邹 – 鄒	灶 – 竈
轩 – 軒	囵 – 圇	饨 – 飩	炀 – 煬
连 – 連	觃 – 覎	饩 – 餼	沣 – 灃
轫 – 軔	帏 – 幃	饪 – 飪	沤 – 漚
【 丨 】	岖 – 嶇	饫 – 飫	沥 – 瀝
卤 – 鹵	岗 – 崗	饬 – 飭	沧 – 滄

沧 – 滄	诏 – 詔	纶 – 綸	择 – 擇
沨 – 渢	译 – 譯	纷 – 紛	茏 – 蘢
沟 – 溝	诒 – 詒	纸 – 紙	苹 – 蘋
沩 – 潙	【一】	纹 – 紋	茑 – 蔦
沪 – 滬	灵 – 靈	纺 – 紡	范 – 範
沈 – 瀋	层 – 層	驴 – 驢	茔 – 塋
忱 – 憮	迟 – 遲	纠 – 糾	荧 – 熒
怀 – 懷	张 – 張	纽 – 紐	荃 – 莖
怄 – 慪	际 – 際	纾 – 紓	枢 – 樞
忧 – 憂	陆 – 陸		枥 – 櫪
忾 – 愾	陇 – 隴	**8 画**	柜 – 櫃
怅 – 悵	陈 – 陳		枫 – 梱
怆 – 愴	坠 – 墜	【一】	枧 – 梘
灾 – 災	陉 – 陘	玮 – 瑋	枨 – 棖
穷 – 窮	妪 – 嫗	环 – 環	板 – 闆
证 – 證	妩 – 嫵	责 – 責	枞 – 樅
诂 – 詁	妫 – 嬀	现 – 現	松 – 鬆
诃 – 訶	刬 – 剗	表 – 錶	枪 – 槍
启 – 啓	劲 – 勁	玱 – 瑲	枫 – 楓
评 – 評	鸡 – 鷄	规 – 規	构 – 構
补 – 補	纬 – 緯	匦 – 匭	杰 – 傑
诅 – 詛	纭 – 紜	拢 – 攏	丧 – 喪
识 – 識	驱 – 驅	拣 – 揀	画 – 畫
诇 – 詗	纯 – 純	垆 – 壚	枣 – 棗
诈 – 詐	纰 – 紕	担 – 擔	卖 – 賣
诉 – 訴	纱 – 紗	顶 – 頂	郁 – 鬱
诊 – 診	纲 – 綱	拥 – 擁	矾 – 礬
诋 – 詆	纳 – 納	势 – 勢	矿 – 礦
诌 – 謅	纴 – 紝	拦 – 攔	砀 – 碭
词 – 詞	驳 – 駁	扛 – 擓	码 – 碼
诎 – 詘	纵 – 縱	拧 – 擰	厕 – 厠
		拨 – 撥	

奋 – 奮	罗 – 羅	侠 – 俠	狞 – 獰
态 – 態	岩 – 巖	侥 – 僥	备 – 備
瓯 – 甌	岽 – 崬	侦 – 偵	枭 – 梟
欧 – 歐	峃 – 嶨	侧 – 側	饯 – 餞
殴 – 毆	帜 – 幟	凭 – 憑	饰 – 飾
垄 – 壟	岭 – 嶺	侨 – 僑	饱 – 飽
郑 – 郟	刿 – 劌	侩 – 儈	饲 – 飼
轰 – 轟	凯 – 凱	货 – 貨	饳 – 飿
顷 – 頃	凯 – 凱	侪 – 儕	饴 – 飴
转 – 轉	峄 – 嶧	侬 – 儂	【丶】
轭 – 軛	败 – 敗	质 – 質	变 – 變
斩 – 斬	账 – 賬	征 – 徵	庞 – 龐
轮 – 輪	贩 – 販	径 – 徑	庙 – 廟
软 – 軟	贬 – 貶	舍 – 捨	疟 – 瘧
鸢 – 鳶	贮 – 貯	刽 – 劊	疠 – 癘
【丨】	图 – 圖	邻 – 鄰	疡 – 瘍
齿 – 齒	购 – 購	怂 – 慫	剂 – 劑
虏 – 虜	【丿】	籴 – 糴	废 – 廢
肾 – 腎	钍 – 釷	觅 – 覓	闸 – 閘
贤 – 賢	钎 – 釬	贪 – 貪	闹 – 鬧
昙 – 曇	钏 – 釧	贫 – 貧	郑 – 鄭
昆 – 崑	钐 – 釤	馂 – 餕	卷 – 捲
崐	钓 – 釣	肤 – 膚	单 – 單
国 – 國	钒 – 釩	肵 – 膊	炜 – 煒
畅 – 暢	钔 – 鍆	肿 – 腫	炝 – 熗
咙 – 嚨	钕 – 釹	胀 – 脹	炉 – 爐
蚬 – 蜆	钖 – 鍚	肮 – 骯	浅 – 淺
鼋 – 黿	钗 – 釵	胁 – 脅	泷 – 瀧
鸣 – 鳴	制 – 製	周 – 週	泸 – 瀘
咛 – 嚀	刮 – 颳	迟 – 邐	泪 – 淚
咝 – 噝	岳 – 嶽	鱼 – 魚	泺 – 濼

注－註
泞－濘
泻－瀉
泼－潑
泽－澤
泾－涇
怜－憐
㤘－㥮
怿－懌
峃－嶨
学－學
宝－寶
宠－寵
审－審
帘－簾
实－實
诓－誆
诔－誄
试－試
诖－詿
诗－詩
诘－詰
诙－詼
诚－誠
郓－鄆
衬－襯
祎－禕
视－視
诛－誅
话－話
诞－誕
诟－詬
诠－詮
诡－詭
询－詢
诣－詣
诤－諍
该－該
详－詳
诧－詫
诨－諢
诩－詡

【乛】

肃－肅
隶－隸
录－録
弥－彌
瀰
陕－陝
驽－駑
驾－駕
参－參
艰－艱
线－綫
绀－紺
绁－紲
绂－紱
练－練
组－組
驵－駔
绅－紳
䌷－紬
细－細
驶－駛
驸－駙
驷－駟
驹－駒
终－終
织－織
驺－騶
绉－縐
驻－駐
绊－絆
驼－駝
绋－紼
绌－絀
绍－紹
驿－驛
绎－繹
经－經
骀－駘
绐－紿
贯－貫

9 画

【一】

贰－貳
帮－幫
珑－瓏
顸－頇
韨－韍
挂－掛
垭－埡
挜－掗
挝－撾
项－項
挞－撻
挟－挾
挠－撓
赵－趙
赍－賫
挡－擋
垲－塏
挢－撟
垫－墊
挤－擠
挥－揮
挦－撏
荐－薦
荚－莢
贳－貰
荛－蕘
荜－蓽
带－帶
茧－繭
荞－蕎
荟－薈
荠－薺
荡－蕩
垩－堊
荣－榮
荤－葷
荥－滎
荦－犖

荧－熒	鸥－鷗	哓－曉	钣－鈑
荨－蕁	龚－龔	哔－嗶	钝－鈍
胡－鬍	残－殘	贵－貴	钞－鈔
荩－藎	殇－殤	虾－蝦	钟－鐘
苏－蘇	轱－軲	蚁－蟻	鍾
荫－蔭	轲－軻	蚂－螞	钡－鋇
荚－莢	轳－轤	虽－雖	钢－鋼
荭－葒	轴－軸	骂－罵	钠－鈉
荮－葤	轶－軼	哕－噦	钥－鑰
药－藥	轷－軤	剐－剮	钦－欽
标－標	轸－軫	郧－鄖	钧－鈞
栈－棧	轹－轢	勋－勛	铃－鈴
栉－櫛	轺－軺	哗－嘩	钨－鎢
栊－櫳	轻－輕	响－響	钩－鈎
栋－棟	鸦－鴉	哙－噲	钪－鈧
栌－櫨	虿－蠆	哝－噥	钫－鈁
栎－櫟	【丨】	哟－喲	钬－鈥
栏－欄	战－戰	峡－峽	钭－鈄
柠－檸	觇－覘	峣－嶢	钮－鈕
柽－檉	点－點	帧－幀	钯－鈀
树－樹	临－臨	罚－罰	毡－氈
鸹－鴰	览－覽	峤－嶠	氢－氫
郦－酈	竖－豎	贱－賤	选－選
咸－鹹	尝－嘗	贴－貼	适－適
砖－磚	眍－瞘	贶－貺	种－種
厘－釐	眬－矓	贻－貽	秋－鞦
砗－硨	哄－閧	【丿】	复－復
砚－硯	闀	钘－鈃	複
砜－碸	哑－啞	钙－鈣	笃－篤
面－麵	显－顯	钚－鈈	俦－儔
牵－牽	哒－噠	钛－鈦	俨－儼

俩 – 倆	侬 – 儂	炼 – 煉	觉 – 覺
俪 – 儷	饼 – 餅	炽 – 熾	宪 – 憲
贷 – 貸	**【丶】**	烁 – 爍	窃 – 竊
顺 – 順	峦 – 巒	烂 – 爛	诚 – 誠
俭 – 儉	弯 – 彎	烃 – 烴	诬 – 誣
剑 – 劍	孪 – 孿	洼 – 窪	语 – 語
鸧 – 鶬	娈 – 孌	洁 – 潔	袄 – 襖
须 – 須	将 – 將	洒 – 灑	诮 – 誚
鬚	奖 – 獎	汰 – 澾	祢 – 禰
胧 – 朧	迹 – 跡	浃 – 浹	误 – 誤
胨 – 腖	蹟	浇 – 澆	诰 – 誥
胪 – 臚	疬 – 癧	浈 – 湞	诱 – 誘
胆 – 膽	疮 – 瘡	浉 – 溮	诲 – 誨
胜 – 勝	疯 – 瘋	浊 – 濁	诳 – 誑
脉 – 脈	亲 – 親	测 – 測	鸩 – 鴆
胫 – 脛	飒 – 颯	浍 – 澮	说 – 說
鸨 – 鴇	闺 – 閨	浏 – 瀏	诵 – 誦
狭 – 狹	闻 – 聞	济 – 濟	诶 – 誒
狮 – 獅	闼 – 闥	浐 – 滻	**【一】**
独 – 獨	闽 – 閩	浑 – 渾	垦 – 墾
狯 – 獪	闾 – 閭	浒 – 滸	昼 – 晝
狱 – 獄	闿 – 闓	浓 – 濃	费 – 費
狲 – 猻	阀 – 閥	浔 – 潯	逊 – 遜
贸 – 貿	阁 – 閣	浕 – 濜	陨 – 隕
饵 – 餌	阐 – 闡	恸 – 慟	险 – 險
饶 – 饒	阂 – 閡	恹 – 懨	贺 – 賀
蚀 – 蝕	养 – 養	恺 – 愷	怼 – 懟
饷 – 餉	姜 – 薑	侧 – 惻	垒 – 壘
饸 – 餄	类 – 類	恼 – 惱	娅 – 婭
饹 – 餎	娄 – 婁	恽 – 惲	娆 – 嬈
饺 – 餃	总 – 總	举 – 舉	娇 – 嬌

绑－綁	载－載	桢－楨	紧－緊
绒－絨	赶－趕	档－檔	党－黨
结－結	盐－鹽	桤－榿	唛－嘜
绔－絝	埘－塒	桥－橋	晒－曬
骁－驍	捆－綑	桦－樺	晓－曉
绕－繞	损－損	桧－檜	唝－嗊
绖－絰	埙－塤	桩－樁	唠－嘮
骄－驕	埚－堝	样－樣	鸭－鴨
骅－驊	捡－撿	贾－賈	唡－啢
绘－繪	赀－貲	逦－邐	晔－曄
骆－駱	挚－摯	唇－脣	晕－暈
骈－駢	热－熱	砺－礪	鸮－鴞
绞－絞	捣－搗	砾－礫	唢－嗩
骇－駭	壶－壺	础－礎	喎－喎
统－統	聂－聶	奢－礱	蚬－蜆
绗－絎	莱－萊	顾－顧	莺－鶯
给－給	莲－蓮	轼－軾	崂－嶗
绚－絢	莳－蒔	轻－輕	崃－崍
绛－絳	莴－萵	轿－轎	罢－罷
络－絡	获－獲	辂－輅	圆－圓
绝－絕	穫	较－較	觊－覬
	莸－蕕	鸫－鶇	贼－賊
10 画	恶－惡	顿－頓	贿－賄
	噁	趸－躉	赂－賂
【一】	劳－蕘	毙－斃	赃－臟
艳－艷	莹－瑩	致－緻	赅－賅
项－項	莺－鶯		赆－贐
珲－琿	鸪－鴣	【丨】	
蚕－蠶	莼－蓴	龀－齔	【丿】
顽－頑	栖－棲	鸬－鸕	钰－鈺
盏－盞	桡－橈	虑－慮	钱－錢
捞－撈		监－監	钲－鉦

钳 – 鉗	称 – 稱	鸳 – 鴛	烩 – 燴
钴 – 鈷	筧 – 筧	皱 – 皺	烬 – 燼
钵 – 鉢	笔 – 筆	饳 – 餑	递 – 遞
钶 – 鈳	笋 – 筍	饿 – 餓	涛 – 濤
钜 – 鉅	债 – 債	馁 – 餒	涝 – 澇
钹 – 鈸	借 – 藉	【丶】	涞 – 淶
钺 – 鉞	倾 – 傾	栾 – 欒	涟 – 漣
钻 – 鑽	赁 – 賃	挛 – 攣	涧 – 澗
钼 – 鉬	顾 – 顧	恋 – 戀	涢
钽 – 鉭	徕 – 徠	桨 – 槳	涡 – 渦
钾 – 鉀	舰 – 艦	浆 – 漿	涂 – 塗
铀 – 鈾	舱 – 艙	席 – 蓆	涤 – 滌
钿 – 鈿	耸 – 聳	症 – 癥	润 – 潤
铁 – 鐵	爱 – 愛	痈 – 癰	涧 – 澗
铂 – 鉑	鸹 – 鴰	斋 – 齋	涨 – 漲
铃 – 鈴	颁 – 頒	痉 – 痙	烫 – 燙
铄 – 鑠	颂 – 頌	准 – 準	涩 – 澀
铅 – 鉛	脍 – 膾	离 – 離	涌 – 湧
铆 – 鉚	脏 – 臟	颃 – 頏	悭 – 慳
铈 – 鈰	髒	资 – 資	悯 – 憫
铉 – 鉉	脐 – 臍	竞 – 競	宽 – 寬
铊 – 鉈	脑 – 腦	阃 – 閫	家 – 傢
铋 – 鉍	胶 – 膠	闽 – 閩	宾 – 賓
铌 – 鈮	脓 – 膿	阄 – 鬮	窍 – 竅
铍 – 鈹	鸥 – 鷗	阅 – 閱	窎 – 寫
铎 – 鐩	玺 – 璽	阆 – 閬	请 – 請
铎 – 鐸	鲂 – 魛	郸 – 鄲	诸 – 諸
氩 – 氬	鸽 – 鴰	烦 – 煩	诹 – 諏
牺 – 犧	狯 – 獪	烧 – 燒	诺 – 諾
敌 – 敵	鸵 – 鴕	烛 – 燭	诼 – 諑
积 – 積	袅 – 裊	烨 – 燁	读 – 讀

诽－誹	绥－綏	营－營	啧－嘖
袜－襪	绦－縧	萦－縈	悬－懸
祯－禎	继－繼	萧－蕭	啭－囀
课－課	绨－綈	萨－薩	跃－躍
诿－諉	骎－駸	梦－夢	啮－嚙
谀－諛	骏－駿	觋－覡	跄－蹌
谁－誰	鸳－鴛	检－檢	蛎－蠣
谂－諗		棂－欞	蛊－蠱
调－調	**11 画**	啬－嗇	蛏－蟶
谄－諂		匮－匱	累－纍
谅－諒	**【一】**	酝－醞	啰－囉
谆－諄	焘－燾	厣－厴	啸－嘯
谇－誶	琏－璉	硕－碩	帻－幘
谈－談	琏－璉	硖－硤	崭－嶄
谊－誼	琐－瑣	硗－磽	逻－邏
谉－譾	麸－麩	砗－硨	帼－幗
	掳－擄	硙－磑	赈－賑
【一】	掴－摑	鸸－鴯	婴－嬰
恳－懇	鸷－鷙	聋－聾	赊－賒
剧－劇	掷－擲	龚－龔	
娲－媧	掸－撣	袭－襲	**【丿】**
娴－嫻	壶－壺	鸶－鷥	铏－鉶
难－難	悫－愨	殒－殞	铐－銬
预－預	据－據	殓－殮	铑－銠
绠－綆	掺－摻	赉－賚	铒－鉺
骊－驪	掼－摜	辄－輒	铓－鋩
绡－綃	职－職	辅－輔	铕－銪
骋－騁	聍－聹	辆－輛	铗－鋏
绢－絹	萚－蘀	堑－塹	铙－鐃
绣－綉	勘－勘		铛－鐺
綉	萝－蘿	**【丨】**	铝－鋁
验－驗	萤－螢	颅－顱	铜－銅

锦 – 錦	债 – 債	鸡 – 鷄	惨 – 慘
铟 – 銦	㑇 – 㑇	旋 – 鏇	惯 – 慣
铠 – 鎧	偿 – 償	阃 – 閫	裤 – 褲
铡 – 鍘	偻 – 僂	阄 – 鬮	谌 – 諶
铢 – 銖	躯 – 軀	阆 – 閬	谋 – 謀
铣 – 銑	皑 – 皚	阅 – 閱	谍 – 諜
铥 – 銩	衅 – 釁	阈 – 閾	谎 – 謊
铤 – 鋌	鸺 – 鵂	阊 – 閶	谏 – 諫
铧 – 鏵	衔 – 銜	阌 – 閿	鞍 – 鞍
铨 – 銓	舻 – 艫	阍 – 閽	谐 – 諧
铢 – 鏿	盘 – 盤	阎 – 閻	谑 – 謔
铪 – 鉿	鸼 – 鵃	羟 – 羥	裆 – 襠
铫 – 銚	龛 – 龕	盖 – 蓋	祸 – 禍
铭 – 銘	鸽 – 鴿	粝 – 糲	谒 – 謁
铬 – 鉻	敛 – 斂	断 – 斷	谓 – 謂
铮 – 錚	领 – 領	兽 – 獸	谔 – 諤
铯 – 銫	胴 – 胴	焖 – 燜	谕 – 諭
铰 – 鉸	脸 – 臉	渍 – 漬	谖 – 諼
铱 – 銥	猎 – 獵	鸿 – 鴻	谗 – 讒
铲 – 鏟	猫 – 貓	渎 – 瀆	谘 – 諮
铳 – 銃	猡 – 玀	渐 – 漸	谙 – 諳
铵 – 銨	猕 – 獼	渑 – 澠	谚 – 諺
银 – 銀	馃 – 餜	渊 – 淵	谛 – 諦
铷 – 銣	馄 – 餛	渔 – 漁	谜 – 謎
矫 – 矯	馅 – 餡	淀 – 澱	谝 – 諞
鸹 – 鴰	馆 – 館	渗 – 滲	谞 – 諝
秸 – 稭	**【丶】**	惬 – 愜	**【一】**
秽 – 穢	鸾 – 鸞	惭 – 慚	弹 – 彈
笺 – 箋	麻 – 蔴	惧 – 懼	堕 – 墮
笼 – 籠	赓 – 賡	惊 – 驚	随 – 隨
筇 – 簹	痒 – 癢	惮 – 憚	粜 – 糶

隐－隱	缀－綴	觌－覿	嵘－嶸
娲－媧	缁－緇	硷－礆	嵚－嶔
婵－嬋		确－確	嵝－嶁
姊－嬸	**12 画**	詟－讋	赋－賦
颇－頗		殚－殫	赌－賭
颈－頸	【一】	颊－頰	赌－賭
绩－績	靓－靚	雳－靂	赎－贖
绪－緒	琼－瓊	辊－輥	赐－賜
绫－綾	辇－輦	辋－輞	赒－賙
骐－騏	鼋－黿	椠－槧	赔－賠
续－續	趋－趨	暂－暫	赕－賧
绮－綺	揽－攬	辍－輟	
骑－騎	颉－頡	辎－輜	【丿】
绯－緋	揿－撳	翘－翹	铸－鑄
绰－綽	搀－攙		锗－鍺
蛰－蟄	蛰－蟄	【丨】	铺－鋪
骒－騍	絷－縶	辈－輩	铼－錸
绲－緄	搁－擱	凿－鑿	铽－鋱
绳－繩	搂－摟	辉－輝	链－鏈
骓－騅	搅－攪	赏－賞	铿－鏗
维－維	联－聯	睐－睞	销－銷
绵－綿	葳－葳	睑－瞼	锁－鎖
绶－綬	葂－蕒	喷－噴	锃－鋥
绷－綳	蒋－蔣	畴－疇	锄－鋤
绸－綢	蒌－蔞	践－踐	锂－鋰
绺－綹	韩－韓	遗－遺	锅－鍋
绻－綣	椟－櫝	蛱－蛺	锆－鋯
综－綜	椤－欏	蛲－蟯	锇－鋨
绽－綻	贲－賁	蛳－螄	锈－銹
绾－綰	椭－橢	蛴－蠐	镥
绿－綠	鹁－鵓	鹃－鵑	锉－銼
骖－驂	鹂－鸝	喽－嘍	锋－鋒

锌－鋅	颍－潁	湿－濕	缅－緬
锎－鐦	飓－颶	溃－潰	缆－纜
锏－鐧	觥－觴	溅－濺	缇－緹
锐－銳	愈－僎	溇－漊	缉－緝
锑－銻	馇－餷	湾－灣	缊－縕
银－銀	馈－饋	谟－謨	缌－緦
锒－鋃	馏－餾	雇－僱	缎－緞
铜－銅	馊－餿	裢－褳	缑－緱
锕－錒	馋－饞	裣－襝	缓－緩
犊－犢	【、】	裤－褲	缒－縋
鸪－鴣	襄－襄	裥－襇	缔－締
鹅－鵝	装－裝	禅－禪	缕－縷
�－頤	蛮－蠻	谠－讜	骗－騙
筑－築	脔－臠	谡－謖	编－編
筚－篳	痨－癆	谢－謝	缗－緡
筛－篩	痫－癇	谣－謠	骚－騷
牍－牘	赓－賡	谤－謗	缘－緣
傥－儻	颏－頦	谥－謚	飨－饗
傧－儐	鹇－鷳	谦－謙	
储－儲	阑－闌	谧－謐	**13 画**
傩－儺	阒－闃	【一】	【一】
惩－懲	阔－闊	属－屬	耢－耮
御－禦	阕－闋	屡－屢	鹉－鵡
颌－頜	粪－糞	骘－騭	鹊－鵲
释－釋	鹈－鵜	疏－疎	韫－韞
鹆－鵒	窜－竄	毵－毿	骛－騖
腊－臘	窝－窩	翚－翬	摄－攝
腘－膕	鹑－鶉	骜－驁	摅－攄
鱿－魷	愤－憤	骘－驂	摆－擺
鲁－魯	愦－憒	缂－緙	罷
鲂－魴	滞－滯	缄－緘	

桢－楨	输－輸	锦－錦	鲐－鮐
摈－擯	【丨】	锧－鑕	颖－穎
毂－轂	频－頻	锨－鍁	鸲－鴝
摊－攤	龃－齟	锫－錇	飑－颮
鹊－鵲	龄－齡	锭－錠	飓－颶
蓝－藍	龅－齙	键－鍵	触－觸
蓦－驀	龆－齠	锯－鋸	雏－雛
鹋－鶓	鉴－鑒	锰－錳	馎－餺
蓟－薊	龊－齪	锱－錙	馍－饃
蒙－矇	嗫－囁	辞－辭	馏－餾
濛	跷－蹺	颏－頦	馐－饈
懞	跸－蹕	穆－穆	【丶】
颐－頤	跻－躋	筹－籌	酱－醬
献－獻	跹－躚	签－簽	鹑－鶉
蓣－蕷	蜗－蝸	籤	痴－癡
榄－欖	嗳－噯	简－簡	瘅－癉
榇－櫬	赗－賵	觎－覦	瘆－瘮
榈－櫚	【丿】	颔－頷	鹧－鷓
楼－樓	锗－鍺	腻－膩	韵－韻
榉－欅	错－錯	鹏－鵬	阖－闔
赖－賴	锘－鍩	腾－騰	阗－闐
碛－磧	锚－錨	鲅－鮁	阙－闕
碍－礙	锛－錛	鲆－鮃	誊－謄
碜－磣	锝－鍀	鲇－鮎	粮－糧
鹌－鵪	锞－錁	鲈－鱸	数－數
尴－尷	锟－錕	鲊－鮓	滟－灩
殨－殨	锡－錫	稣－穌	溇－潊
雾－霧	锢－錮	鲋－鮒	满－滿
辌－輬	锣－鑼	鲫－鰤	滤－濾
辐－輻	锤－錘	鲍－鮑	滥－濫
辑－輯	锥－錐	鲅－鮁	滗－潷

滦 – 灤	缡 – 縭	辕 – 轅	锻 – 鍛
漓 – 灕	缢 – 縊	辖 – 轄	锼 – 鎪
滨 – 濱	缣 – 縑	辗 – 輾	锾 – 鍰
滩 – 灘	缤 – 繽	【丨】	锵 – 鏘
溆 – 漵	骗 – 騙	龇 – 齜	锿 – 鎄
慑 – 懾	**14 画**	龈 – 齦	镀 – 鍍
誉 – 譽		鹃 – 鵑	镁 – 鎂
鲎 – 鱟	【一】	颗 – 顆	镂 – 鏤
骞 – 騫	瑷 – 璦	瞄 – 瞜	镃 – 鎡
寝 – 寢	赘 – 贅	暖 – 曖	镄 – 鐨
窥 – 窺	觏 – 覯	鹖 – 鶡	锔 – 錒
窦 – 竇	韬 – 韜	踌 – 躊	鹙 – 鶖
谨 – 謹	叆 – 靉	踊 – 踴	稳 – 穩
谩 – 謾	墙 – 牆	蜡 – 蠟	簣 – 簣
谪 – 謫	撄 – 攖	蜗 – 蝸	箧 – 篋
谫 – 譾	蔷 – 薔	蝇 – 蠅	箨 – 籜
谬 – 謬	蔌 – 蔌	蝉 – 蟬	箩 – 籮
【一】	蔹 – 薟	鹗 – 鶚	箪 – 簞
辟 – 闢	蔟 – 蔟	嘤 – 嚶	箓 – 籙
缓 – 緩	蔺 – 藺	罴 – 羆	舆 – 輿
嫔 – 嬪	蔼 – 藹	赙 – 賻	膑 – 臏
缙 – 縉	鹕 – 鶘	罂 – 罌	鲑 – 鮭
缜 – 縝	槚 – 檟	赚 – 賺	鲒 – 鮚
缚 – 縛	槛 – 檻	鹘 – 鶻	鲔 – 鮪
缛 – 縟	槟 – 檳	【丿】	鲖 – 鮦
辔 – 轡	楮 – 櫧	锲 – 鍥	鲗 – 鰂
缝 – 縫	酽 – 釅	锴 – 鍇	鲙 – 鱠
骝 – 騮	酾 – 釃	锶 – 鍶	鲚 – 鱭
缡 – 縭	酿 – 釀	锷 – 鍔	鲛 – 鮫
缟 – 縞	霁 – 霽	锹 – 鍬	鲜 – 鮮
缠 – 纏	愿 – 願	锸 – 鍤	
	殡 – 殯		

鲟 - 鱘
飏 - 颺
馑 - 饉
馒 - 饅

【、】

銮 - 鑾
瘗 - 瘞
瘘 - 瘻
阆 - 閬
羞 - 羞
誊 - 謄
糁 - 糝
鹚 - 鶿
潇 - 瀟
潋 - 瀲
潍 - 濰
赛 - 賽
窦 - 竇
谭 - 譚
谮 - 譖
禛 - 禩
褛 - 褸
谯 - 譙
谰 - 讕
谱 - 譜
谲 - 譎

【一】

鹛 - 鶥
嫱 - 嬙
骛 - 鶩
缥 - 縹

骠 - 驃
缦 - 縵
骡 - 騾
缧 - 縲
缨 - 纓
骢 - 驄
缩 - 縮
缪 - 繆
缫 - 繅

15 画

【一】

楼 - 樓
璎 - 瓔
䃅 - 䃸
撵 - 攆
撷 - 擷
撺 - 攛
聩 - 聵
聪 - 聰
觐 - 覲
鞑 - 韃
鞒 - 鞽
蕲 - 蘄
赜 - 賾
蕴 - 蘊
樯 - 檣
樱 - 櫻
飘 - 飄
靥 - 靨
魇 - 魘

餍 - 饜
霉 - 黴
辘 - 轆

【丨】

龉 - 齬
龊 - 齪
觑 - 覷
瞒 - 瞞
题 - 題
颙 - 顒
踬 - 躓
踯 - 躑
蝾 - 蠑
蝼 - 螻
噜 - 嚕
嘱 - 囑
颛 - 顓

【丿】

镊 - 鑷
镇 - 鎮
镉 - 鎘
锐 - 銳
镏 - 鎦
镍 - 鎳
锋 - 鋒
镏 - 鎦
镐 - 鎬
镑 - 鎊
镒 - 鎰
镓 - 鎵
镔 - 鑌

镝 - 鏑
簀 - 簀
篓 - 簍
鹠 - 鶹
鹙 - 鶖
鹝 - 鶪
鲠 - 鯁
鲡 - 鱺
鲢 - 鰱
鲣 - 鰹
鲥 - 鰣
鲤 - 鯉
鲦 - 鰷
鲧 - 鯀
鲩 - 鯇
卿 - 鄕
徼 - 徼
馔 - 饌

【、】

瘪 - 癟
瘫 - 癱
齑 - 齏
颜 - 顏
鹣 - 鶼
鲨 - 鯊
澜 - 瀾
额 - 額
谳 - 讞
褴 - 襤
遣 - 譴
鹤 - 鶴

谵 – 譫

【一】

屡 – 屢

缬 – 纈

缭 – 繚

缮 – 繕

缯 – 繒

16 画

【一】

糯 – 糯

擞 – 擻

颞 – 顳

颟 – 顢

薮 – 藪

颠 – 顛

橹 – 櫓

橼 – 櫞

鹥 – 鷖

赝 – 贗

飙 – 飆

獭 – 獺

錾 – 鏨

辙 – 轍

辚 – 轔

【丨】

蹉 – 蹉

螨 – 蟎

鹦 – 鸚

赠 – 贈

【丿】

锗 – 鍺

镖 – 鏢

镗 – 鏜

镘 – 鏝

镙 – 鏍

镛 – 鏞

镜 – 鏡

镝 – 鏑

镞 – 鏃

氇 – 氌

赞 – 贊

穑 – 穡

篮 – 籃

篱 – 籬

魉 – 魉

鲭 – 鯖

鲮 – 鯪

鲰 – 鯫

鲱 – 鯡

鲲 – 鯤

鲳 – 鯧

鲵 – 鯢

鲶 – 鯰

鲷 – 鯛

鲸 – 鯨

鲻 – 鯔

獭 – 獺

【丶】

鹧 – 鷓

瘿 – 癭

瘾 – 癮

斓 – 斕

辩 – 辯

濑 – 瀨

濒 – 瀕

懒 – 懶

黉 – 黌

【一】

鹨 – 鷚

颖 – 穎

缰 – 繮

缱 – 繾

缲 – 繰

缳 – 繯

缴 – 繳

17 画

【一】

薛 – 薛

鹩 – 鷯

【丨】

龋 – 齲

龌 – 齷

瞩 – 矚

蹒 – 蹣

蹑 – 躡

蟏 – 蠨

嚓 – 嚇

羁 – 羈

赡 – 贍

【丿】

镢 – 鐝

镣 – 鐐

镤 – 鏷

镥 – 鑥

镦 – 鐓

镧 – 鑭

镨 – 鐠

镩 – 鑹

镪 – 鏹

镫 – 鐙

簖 – 籪

鹪 – 鷦

鲭 – 鰆

鲽 – 鰈

鳌 – 鰵

鳃 – 鰓

鳀 – 鯷

鳄 – 鰐

鳅 – 鰍

鳆 – 鰒

鳇 – 鰉

鳈 – 鰁

鳊 – 鯿

【丶】

鹫 – 鷲

辫 – 辮

赢 – 贏

懑 – 懣

【一】

鹬 – 鷸

骤 – 驟

18 画

【一】

鳌 – 鰲
鞑 – 韃
靥 – 靨

【丨】

歔 – 歔
颗 – 顆
鹭 – 鷺
嚣 – 囂
髅 – 髏

【丿】

镬 – 鑊
镭 – 鐳
镮 – 鐶
镯 – 鐲
镰 – 鐮
镱 – 鐿
雠 – 讎
䲢 – 䲢
鳍 – 鰭
鳎 – 鰨
鳏 – 鰥
鳑 – 鰟
鳒 – 鰜

【丶】

鹫 – 鷲
鹰 – 鷹
癫 – 癲
鞯 – 韉
谶 – 讖

【乛】

鸥 – 鷗

19 画

【一】

攒 – 攢
霭 – 靄

【丨】

鳖 – 鱉
蹿 – 躥
巅 – 巔
髋 – 髖
髌 – 髕

【丿】

镲 – 鑔
簖 – 籪
鳘 – 鰵
鳓 – 鰳
鳔 – 鰾
鳕 – 鱈

鳗 – 鰻
鳙 – 鱅
鳛 – 鰼

【丶】

颤 – 顫
癣 – 癬
谵 – 譫

【乛】

骥 – 驥
缵 – 纘

20 画

【一】

瓒 – 瓚
鬓 – 鬢
颟 – 顢

【丨】

鼍 – 鼉
黩 – 黷

【丿】

镳 – 鑣
镴 – 鑞
臜 – 臢
鳜 – 鱖
鳝 – 鱔
鳞 – 鱗

鳟 – 鱒

【乛】

骧 – 驤

21 画

鞿 – 韁
躏 – 躪
鳢 – 鱧
鳣 – 鱣
癞 – 癩
赣 – 贛
灏 – 灝

22 画

鹳 – 鸛
镶 – 鑲

23 画

趱 – 趲
颧 – 顴
躜 – 躦

25 画

镢 – 钁
馕 – 饢
戆 – 戇

From Traditional to Simplified Characters

繁簡對照

Radicals
簡化偏旁

丫
愛 – 爱

ㄅ
罷 – 罢
貝 – 贝
備 – 备
筆 – 笔
畢 – 毕
邊 – 边
賓 – 宾

ㄘ
參 – 参
倉 – 仓
產 – 产
嘗 – 尝
長 – 长
車 – 车
齒 – 齿
蟲 – 虫
芻 – 刍
從 – 从
竄 – 窜

ㄉ
達 – 达
帶 – 带
單 – 单
當、噹 – 当
黨 – 党
東 – 东
動 – 动
斷 – 断
對 – 对
隊 – 队

ㄜ
爾 – 尔

ㄈ
發、髮 – 发
豐 – 丰
風 – 风

ㄍ
岡 – 冈
廣 – 广
歸 – 归

龜 – 龟
國 – 国
過 – 过

ㄏ
華 – 华
畫 – 画
匯、彙 – 汇
會 – 会

ㄐ
幾 – 几
夾 – 夹
戔 – 戋
監 – 监
薦 – 荐
見 – 见
將 – 将
節 – 节
盡、儘 – 尽
進 – 进
舉 – 举
車 – 车

ㄎ
殼 – 壳
會 – 会

ㄌ
來 – 来
樂 – 乐
離 – 离
歷、曆 – 历
麗 – 丽
兩 – 两
靈 – 灵
劉 – 刘
龍 – 龙
婁 – 娄
盧 – 卢
虜 – 虏
鹵、滷 – 卤
錄 – 录
慮 – 虑
侖 – 仑
羅、囉 – 罗

ㄇ

馬 – 马
買 – 买
賣 – 卖
麥 – 麦
門 – 门
黽 – 黾

ㄋ

難 – 难
鳥 – 鸟
聶 – 聂
寧 – 宁
農 – 农

ㄛ

區 – 区

ㄑ

齊 – 齐
豈 – 岂
氣 – 气
遷 – 迁
僉 – 佥
喬 – 乔

殼 – 壳
親 – 亲
窮 – 穷
區 – 区

ㄙ

嗇 – 啬
參 – 参
殺 – 杀
審 – 审
聖 – 圣
師 – 师
時 – 时
壽 – 寿
屬 – 属
雙 – 双
肅 – 肃
歲 – 岁
孫 – 孙

ㄊ

條 – 条

ㄨ

萬 – 万

爲 – 为
韋 – 韦
烏 – 乌
無 – 无

ㄒ

獻 – 献
鄉 – 乡
寫 – 写
尋 – 寻

ㄧ

亞 – 亚
嚴 – 严
厭 – 厌
堯 – 尧
頁 – 页
業 – 业
義 – 义
藝 – 艺
陰 – 阴
隱 – 隐
猶 – 犹
魚 – 鱼
與 – 与

樂 – 乐
雲 – 云

ㄗ

長 – 长
鄭 – 郑
執 – 执
質 – 质
專 – 专

简化偏旁

言 – 讠
食 – 饣
昜 – 旸
糹 – 纟
臤 – 収
戀 – 䜌
臨 – 临
戠 – 只
金 – 钅
與 – 兴
罒 – 罕
坙 – 圣
戀 – 亦
咼 – 呙

Zhu Yin Index
註音字母索引

瀕 – 濒
鬢 – 鬓
擯 – 摈
殯 – 殡
臏 – 膑
髕 – 髌

ㄅㄧㄥ

檳 – 槟
餅 – 饼

ㄅㄛ

餑 – 饽
缽 – 钵
撥 – 拨
鵓 – 鹁
餺 – 博
鈸 – 钹
駁 – 驳
鉑 – 铂
蔔 – 卜

ㄅㄨ

補 – 补
鈽 – 钚

ㄊ

ㄊㄞ

纔 – 才
財 – 财

ㄊㄢ

參 – 参
驂 – 骖
蠶 – 蚕
慚 – 惭

殘 – 残
慘 – 惨
穇 – 穇
燦 – 灿

ㄊㄤ

倉 – 仓
滄 – 沧
蒼 – 苍
傖 – 伧
鶬 – 鸧
艙 – 舱

ㄊㄜ

測 – 测
惻 – 恻
厠 – 厕
側 – 侧

ㄊㄣ

參 – 参

ㄊㄥ

層 – 层

ㄔㄚ

馇 – 馇
鍤 – 锸
鑔 – 镲
詫 – 诧

ㄔㄞ

釵 – 钗
儕 – 侪
蠆 – 虿

ㄔㄢ

攙 – 搀

摻 – 掺
纏 – 缠
禪 – 禅
蟬 – 蝉
嬋 – 婵
讒 – 谗
饞 – 馋
産 – 产
滻 – 浐
鏟 – 铲
蔵 – 蒇
闡 – 阐
囅 – 冁
諂 – 谄
顫 – 颤
懺 – 忏
剗 – 刬

ㄔㄤ

倀 – 伥
閶 – 阊
鯧 – 鲳
嘗 – 尝
償 – 偿
鱨 – 鲿
長 – 长
腸 – 肠
場 – 场
廠 – 厂
悵 – 怅
暢 – 畅

ㄔㄠ

鈔 – 钞

ㄔㄜ

車 – 车
硨 – 砗
徹 – 彻

ㄔㄣ

諶 – 谌
塵 – 尘
陳 – 陈
磣 – 碜
櫬 – 梫
襯 – 衬
讖 – 谶
稱 – 称
齔 – 龀

ㄔㄥ

檉 – 柽
蟶 – 蛏
鐺 – 铛
䫆 – 桢
稱 – 称
棖 – 枨
誠 – 诚
懲 – 惩
騁 – 骋

ㄔ

鷗 – 鸥
遲 – 迟
馳 – 驰
齒 – 齿
熾 – 炽

飭 – 饬	瘡 – 疮	躐 – 蹿	誕 – 诞
ㄔㄨㄥ	闖 – 闯	鑹 – 镩	**ㄉㄤ**
衝 – 冲	愴 – 怆	攢 – 攒	襠 – 裆
蟲 – 虫	創 – 创	竄 – 窜	鐺 – 铛
寵 – 宠	**ㄔㄨㄟ**	**ㄘㄨㄟ**	當,噹 – 当
銃 – 铳	錘 – 锤	縗 – 缞	黨 – 党
ㄔㄡ	**ㄔㄨㄣ**	**ㄘㄨㄛ**	讜 – 谠
紬 – 䌷	鰆 – 鰆	鹺 – 鹾	擋 – 挡
疇 – 畴	鶉 – 鹑	錯 – 错	檔 – 档
籌 – 筹	純 – 纯	銼 – 锉	碭 – 砀
躊 – 踌	蒓 – 莼	**ㄉ**	蕩 – 荡
儔 – 俦	**ㄔㄨㄛ**	**ㄉㄚ**	**ㄉㄠ**
雔 – 雠	綽 – 绰	達 – 达	魛 – 鱽
綢 – 绸	齱 – 龊	噠 – 哒	禱 – 祷
醜 – 丑	輟 – 辍	韃 – 鞑	島 – 岛
ㄔㄨ	**ㄘ**	**ㄉㄞ**	搗 – 捣
齣 – 出	鷀 – 鹚	貸 – 贷	導 – 导
鋤 – 锄	辭 – 辞	給 – 给	**ㄉㄜ**
芻 – 刍	詞 – 词	帶 – 带	鍀 – 锝
雛 – 雏	賜 – 赐	瓅 – 瓂	**ㄉㄥ**
儲 – 储	**ㄘㄨㄥ**	**ㄉㄢ**	燈 – 灯
礎 – 础	聰 – 聪	單 – 单	鐙 – 镫
處 – 处	驄 – 骢	擔 – 担	鄧 – 邓
絀 – 绌	樅 – 枞	殫 – 殚	**ㄉㄧ**
觸 – 触	蓯 – 苁	簞 – 箪	鏑 – 镝
ㄔㄨㄞ	從 – 从	鄲 – 郸	覿 – 觌
圌 – 闿	叢 – 丛	膽 – 胆	糴 – 籴
ㄔㄨㄢ	**ㄘㄡ**	賧 – 赕	敵 – 敌
傳 – 传	輳 – 辏	憚 – 惮	滌 – 涤
釧 – 钏	**ㄘㄨㄢ**	癉 – 瘅	詆 – 诋
ㄔㄨㄤ	攛 – 撺	彈 – 弹	諦 – 谛

締–缔	東–东	隊–队	鴯–鸸
遞–递	鶇–鸫	**ㄉㄨㄣ**	餌–饵
ㄉㄧㄢ	崠–崬	噸–吨	鉺–铒
顛–颠	鼕–冬	鐓–镦	爾–尔
癲–癫	動–动	蹾–趸	邇–迩
巔–巅	凍–冻	鈍–钝	貳–贰
點–点	棟–栋	頓–顿	**ㄈ**
澱–淀	腖–胨	**ㄉㄨㄛ**	**ㄈㄚ**
墊–垫	**ㄉㄡ**	奪–夺	發、髮–发
電–电	鈄–钭	鐸–铎	罰–罚
鈿–钿	鬥–斗	馱–驮	閥–阀
ㄉㄧㄠ	竇–窦	墮–堕	**ㄈㄢ**
鯛–鲷	**ㄉㄨ**	飿–饳	煩–烦
銚–铫	讀–读	**ㄜ**	礬–矾
錭–铞	瀆–渎	**ㄜ**	釩–钒
窵–窎	櫝–椟	額–额	販–贩
釣–钓	黷–黩	鋨–锇	飯–饭
調–调	犢–犊	鵝–鹅	範–范
ㄉㄧㄝ	牘–牍	訛–讹	**ㄈㄤ**
諜–谍	獨–独	惡、噁–恶	鈁–钫
鰈–鲽	賭–赌	堊–垩	魴–鲂
絰–绖	篤–笃	軛–轭	訪–访
叠–迭	鍍–镀	諤–谔	紡–纺
ㄉㄧㄥ	**ㄉㄨㄢ**	鶚–鹗	**ㄈㄟ**
釘–钉	斷–断	鱷–鳄	緋–绯
頂–顶	鍛–锻	鍔–锷	鯡–鲱
訂–订	緞–缎	餓–饿	飛–飞
錠–锭	籪–簖	**ㄝ**	誹–诽
ㄉㄧㄡ	**ㄉㄨㄟ**	誒–诶	廢–废
銩–铥	懟–怼	**ㄦ**	費–费
ㄉㄨㄥ	對–对	兒–儿	鐨–镄

ㄈㄣ
纷 – 纷
墳 – 坟
豶 – 豮
糞 – 粪
憤 – 愤
僨 – 偾
奮 – 奋

ㄈㄥ
豐 – 丰
灃 – 沣
鋒 – 锋
風 – 风
渢 – 沨
瘋 – 疯
楓 – 枫
碸 – 砜
馮 – 冯
縫 – 缝
諷 – 讽
鳳 – 凤
賵 – 赗

ㄈㄨ
麩 – 麸
膚 – 肤
輻 – 辐
韍 – 韨
紱 – 绂
鳧 – 凫
紼 – 绋
輔 – 辅

撫 – 抚
賦 – 赋
賻 – 赙
縛 – 缚
訃 – 讣
復、複、覆 –
　　复
鰒 – 鳆
駙 – 驸
鮒 – 鲋
負 – 负
婦 – 妇

ㄍ

ㄍㄚ
釓 – 钆

ㄍㄞ
該 – 该
賅 – 赅
蓋 – 盖
鈣 – 钙

ㄍㄢ
乾、幹 – 干
尷 – 尴
趕 – 赶
贛 – 赣
紺 – 绀

ㄍㄤ
岡 – 冈
剛 – 刚
棡 – 㭎
綱 – 纲

鋼 – 钢
摃 – 扛
崗 – 岗

ㄍㄠ
鎬 – 镐
縞 – 缟
誥 – 诰
鋯 – 锆

ㄍㄜ
鴿 – 鸽
擱 – 搁
鎘 – 镉
頜 – 颌
閣 – 阁
個 – 个
鉻 – 铬

ㄍㄟ
給 – 给

ㄍㄥ
賡 – 赓
鶊 – 鹒
鯁 – 鲠
綆 – 绠

ㄍㄨㄥ
龔 – 龚
鞏 – 巩
貢 – 贡
嗊 – 唝

ㄍㄡ
緱 – 缑
溝 – 沟

鈎 – 钩
覯 – 觏
訽 – 诟
構 – 构
購 – 购

ㄍㄨ
軲 – 轱
鴣 – 鸪
詁 – 诂
鈷 – 钴
賈 – 贾
蠱 – 蛊
轂 – 毂
餶 – 馉
鶻 – 鹘
穀 – 谷
鵠 – 鹄
顧 – 顾
錮 – 锢

ㄍㄨㄚ
颳 – 刮
鴰 – 鸹
剮 – 剐
詿 – 诖

ㄍㄨㄢ
關 – 关
綸 – 纶
鰥 – 鳏
觀 – 观
館 – 馆
鸛 – 鹳

貫 – 贯	蟈 – 蝈	鶹 – 鹠	華 – 华
慣 – 惯	國 – 国	頜 – 颌	驊 – 骅
摜 – 掼	摑 – 掴	餄 – 饸	嘩 – 哗
《ㄨㄤ	幗 – 帼	閤 – 合	鏵 – 铧
廣 – 广	馃 – 馃	紇 – 纥	畫 – 画
獷 – 犷	膕 – 腘	鶴 – 鹤	嬅 – 婳
《ㄨㄟ	過 – 过	賀 – 贺	劃 – 划
媧 – 妫	厂	嚇 – 吓	樺 – 桦
潙 – 沩	厂ㄚ	厂ㄥ	話 – 话
規 – 规	鉿 – 铪	鵿 – 䳭	厂ㄨㄞ
鮭 – 鲑	厂ㄞ	厂ㄨㄥ	懷 – 怀
閨 – 闺	還 – 还	轟 – 轰	壞 – 坏
歸 – 归	駭 – 骇	矕 – 黉	厂ㄨㄢ
龜 – 龟	厂ㄢ	鴻 – 鸿	歡 – 欢
軌 – 轨	頇 – 顸	紅 – 红	還 – 还
甌 – 瓯	韓 – 韩	葒 – 荭	環 – 环
詭 – 诡	闞 – 阚	訌 – 讧	繯 – 缳
鱖 – 鳜	嘾 – 㘎	厂ㄡ	鐶 – 镮
櫃 – 柜	漢 – 汉	後 – 后	緩 – 缓
貴 – 贵	頷 – 颔	鱟 – 鲎	鯇 – 鲩
劌 – 刿	厂ㄤ	厂ㄨ	厂ㄨㄤ
檜 – 桧	絎 – 绗	軒 – 轩	鰉 – 鳇
劊 – 刽	頏 – 颃	壺 – 壶	謊 – 谎
《ㄨㄣ	厂ㄠ	鬍 – 胡	厂ㄨㄟ
輥 – 辊	顥 – 颢	鶘 – 鹕	揮 – 挥
緄 – 绲	灝 – 灏	鵠 – 鹄	輝 – 辉
鯤 – 鲲	號 – 号	鶻 – 鹘	翬 – 翚
《ㄨㄛ	厂ㄜ	滸 – 浒	詼 – 诙
渦 – 涡	訶 – 诃	滬 – 沪	迴 – 回
堝 – 埚	閤 – 阁	護 – 护	匯、彙 – 汇
鍋 – 锅	闔 – 阖	厂ㄨㄚ	賄 – 贿

穭－秽	機－机	ㄐㄧㄚ	揀－拣
會－会	饑－饥	傢－家	筧－笕
燴－烩	譏－讥	鎵－镓	繭－茧
薈－荟	璣－玑	夾－夹	檢－检
繪－绘	磯－矶	浹－浃	撿－捡
誨－诲	嘰－叽	頰－颊	瞼－睑
殨－殨	鶏－鸡	荚－荚	儉－俭
諱－讳	鵜－鹡	蛺－蛱	褲－裥
ㄏㄨㄣ	輯－辑	鋏－铗	簡－简
葷－荤	極－极	郟－郏	諫－谏
闇－阍	級－级	賈－贾	漸－渐
渾－浑	擠－挤	檟－槚	檻－槛
琿－珲	給－给	鉀－钾	賤－贱
餛－馄	幾－几	價－价	濺－溅
諢－诨	蟣－虮	駕－驾	踐－践
ㄏㄨㄛ	濟－济	ㄐㄧㄢ	餞－饯
鈥－钬	霽－霁	鶼－鹣	薦－荐
夥－伙	薺－荠	鰜－鳒	鑒－鉴
鑊－镬	劑－剂	縑－缣	見－见
獲、穫－获	鱭－鲚	戔－戋	梘－枧
禍－祸	際－际	箋－笺	艦－舰
貨－货	績－绩	堅－坚	劍－剑
ㄐ	計－计	鰹－鲣	鍵－键
ㄐㄧ	繫－系	缄－缄	澗－涧
齏－齑	驥－骥	韉－鞯	鐧－锏
躋－跻	覬－觊	監－监	ㄐㄧㄤ
擊－击	薊－蓟	殲－歼	薑－姜
賫－赍	鯽－鲫	艱－艰	將－将
緝－缉	記－记	間－间	槳－桨
積－积	紀－纪	諫－谏	疆－疆
羈－羁	繼－继	鹼－硷	講－讲

漿 – 浆
獎 – 奖
蔣 – 蒋
醬 – 酱
絳 – 绛

ㄐㄧㄠ

膠 – 胶
鮫 – 鲛
鵁 – 鸡
澆 – 浇
驕 – 骄
嬌 – 娇
鷦 – 鹪
餃 – 饺
鉸 – 铰
絞 – 绞
僥 – 侥
矯 – 矫
攪 – 搅
繳 – 缴
覺 – 觉
較 – 较
轎 – 轿
撟 – 挢
嶠 – 峤

ㄐㄧㄝ

階 – 阶
癤 – 疖
訐 – 讦
潔 – 洁
詰 – 诘

擷 – 撷
頡 – 颉
結 – 结
鮚 – 鲒
節 – 节
藉 – 借
誡 – 诫

ㄐㄧㄣ

謹 – 谨
饉 – 馑
覲 – 觐
緊 – 紧
錦 – 锦
僅 – 仅
勁 – 劲
進 – 进
璡 – 琎
縉 – 缙
盡、儘 – 尽
濜 – 浕
蓋 – 荩
贐 – 赆
燼 – 烬

ㄐㄧㄥ

驚 – 惊
鯨 – 鲸
鶄 – 鹊
涇 – 泾
莖 – 茎
經 – 经
頸 – 颈

剄 – 刭
鏡 – 镜
競 – 竞
痙 – 痉
勁 – 劲
脛 – 胫
徑 – 径
靚 – 靓

ㄐㄧㄡ

糾 – 纠
鳩 – 鸠
鬮 – 阄
鷲 – 鹫
舊 – 旧

ㄐㄩ

車 – 车
駒 – 驹
鶋 – 鹍
鋦 – 锔
舉 – 举
齟 – 龃
櫸 – 榉
詎 – 讵
懼 – 惧
颶 – 飓
窶 – 窭
屨 – 屦
據 – 据
劇 – 剧
鋸 – 锯

ㄐㄩㄢ

鵑 – 鹃
鐫 – 镌
捲 – 卷
絹 – 绢

ㄐㄩㄝ

覺 – 觉
鐝 – 镢
钁 – 镢
譎 – 谲
訣 – 诀
絕 – 绝

ㄐㄩㄣ

軍 – 军
皸 – 皲
鈞 – 钧
駿 – 骏

ㄎ

ㄎㄞ

開 – 开
鐦 – 锎
愷 – 恺
塏 – 垲
剴 – 剀
鎧 – 铠
凱 – 凯
闓 – 闿
鍇 – 锴
愾 – 忾

ㄎㄢ

龕 – 龛
檻 – 槛

楞 – 崚	礫 – 砾	臉 – 脸	臨 – 临
ㄌㄜ	歷、曆 – 历	戀 – 恋	鄰 – 邻
鰳 – 鳓	瀝 – 沥	鏈 – 链	藺 – 蔺
樂 – 乐	壢 – 坜	煉 – 炼	躪 – 躏
餎 – 饹	癧 – 疬	練 – 练	賃 – 赁
ㄌㄟ	靂 – 雳	瀲 – 潋	**ㄌㄧㄥ**
鐳 – 镭	櫪 – 枥	殮 – 殓	鯪 – 鲮
纍 – 累	藶 – 苈	襝 – 裣	綾 – 绫
縲 – 缧	嚦 – 呖	褳 – 裢	齡 – 龄
誄 – 诔	癘 – 疠	**ㄌㄧㄤ**	鈴 – 铃
壘 – 垒	糲 – 粝	糧 – 粮	鴒 – 鸰
類 – 类	礪 – 砺	兩 – 两	靈 – 灵
ㄌㄧ	蠣 – 蛎	倆 – 俩	欞 – 棂
離 – 离	櫟 – 栎	啢 – 唡	領 – 领
灕 – 漓	轢 – 轹	魎 – 魉	嶺 – 岭
籬 – 篱	隸 – 隶	諒 – 谅	**ㄌㄧㄡ**
縭 – 缡	**ㄌㄧㄚ**	輛 – 辆	飀 – 飗
驪 – 骊	倆 – 俩	**ㄌㄧㄠ**	劉 – 刘
鸝 – 鹂	**ㄌㄧㄢ**	鷯 – 鹩	瀏 – 浏
鱺 – 鲡	簾 – 帘	繚 – 缭	驑 – 骝
禮 – 礼	鐮 – 镰	療 – 疗	鎦 – 镏
邐 – 逦	聯 – 联	遼 – 辽	綹 – 绺
裏 – 里	連 – 连	瞭 – 了	餾 – 馏
鋰 – 锂	漣 – 涟	釕 – 钌	鷚 – 鹨
鯉 – 鲤	蓮 – 莲	鐐 – 镣	陸 – 陆
鱧 – 鳢	鰱 – 鲢	**ㄌㄧㄝ**	**ㄌㄨㄥ**
麗 – 丽	璉 – 琏	獵 – 猎	龍 – 龙
儷 – 俪	奩 – 奁	鴷 – 䴕	瀧 – 泷
酈 – 郦	憐 – 怜	**ㄌㄧㄣ**	瓏 – 珑
厲 – 厉	斂 – 敛	轔 – 辚	聾 – 聋
勵 – 励	蘞 – 蔹	鱗 – 鳞	櫳 – 栊

礱 – 砻
籠 – 笼
蘢 – 茏
嚨 – 咙
曨 – 昽
朧 – 胧
壟 – 垄
攏 – 拢
隴 – 陇

ㄌㄡ

瞜 – 䁖
婁 – 娄
僂 – 偻
嘍 – 喽
樓 – 楼
漊 – 溇
蔞 – 蒌
髏 – 髅
嶁 – 嵝
耬 – 耧
摟 – 搂
嶁 – 嵝
簍 – 篓
瘻 – 瘘
鏤 – 镂

ㄌㄨ

嚕 – 噜
廬 – 庐
爐 – 炉
蘆 – 芦
盧 – 卢

瀘 – 泸
壚 – 垆
櫨 – 栌
顱 – 颅
鸕 – 鸬
臚 – 胪
鱸 – 鲈
鑪 – 舻
鹵、滷 – 卤
虜 – 虏
擄 – 掳
魯 – 鲁
櫓 – 橹
鐪 – 镥
轆 – 辘
輅 – 辂
賂 – 赂
鷺 – 鹭
陸 – 陆
錄 – 录
籙 – 箓
綠 – 绿
轤 – 轳
氌 – 氇

ㄌㄩ

驢 – 驴
閭 – 闾
梱 – 榈
屢 – 屡
僂 – 偻
褸 – 褛

縷 – 缕
鋁 – 铝
慮 – 虑
濾 – 滤
綠 – 绿

ㄌㄩㄢ

孌 – 娈
欒 – 栾
灤 – 滦
巒 – 峦
臠 – 脔
鑾 – 銮
挛 – 挛
鸞 – 鸾
孿 – 孪
亂 – 乱

ㄌㄩㄣ

掄 – 抡
侖 – 仑
淪 – 沦
輪 – 轮
圇 – 囵
綸 – 纶
倫 – 伦
論 – 论

ㄌㄨㄛ

騾 – 骡
腡 – 脶
羅、囉 – 罗
邏 – 逻
蘿 – 萝

鑼 – 锣
籮 – 箩
欏 – 椤
玀 – 猡
犖 – 荦
濼 – 泺
駱 – 骆
絡 – 络

ㄇ

ㄇ

嘸 – 呒

ㄇㄚ

媽 – 妈
馬 – 马
螞 – 蚂
瑪 – 玛
碼 – 码
獁 – 犸
罵 – 骂
嗎 – 吗
嗎 – 唛

ㄇㄞ

買 – 买
麥 – 麦
賣 – 卖
邁 – 迈
賈 – 荬

ㄇㄢ

顢 – 颟
饅 – 馒
鰻 – 鳗

蠻 – 蛮	錳 – 锰	銘 – 铭	訥 – 讷
瞞 – 瞒	夢 – 梦	ㄇㄧㄡ	ㄋㄟ
滿 – 满	ㄇㄧ	謬 – 谬	餒 – 馁
蟎 – 螨	謎 – 谜	繆 – 缪	ㄋㄧ
謾 – 谩	禰 – 祢	ㄇㄛ	鯢 – 鲵
縵 – 缦	彌、瀰 – 弥	謨 – 谟	鈮 – 铌
鏝 – 镘	獼 – 猕	饃 – 馍	擬 – 拟
ㄇㄤ	謐 – 谧	驀 – 蓦	膩 – 腻
鋩 – 铓	覓 – 觅	ㄇㄡ	ㄋㄧㄢ
ㄇㄠ	ㄇㄧㄢ	謀 – 谋	鮎 – 鲇
錨 – 锚	綿 – 绵	繆 – 缪	鯰 – 鲶
鉚 – 铆	澠 – 渑	ㄇㄨ	輦 – 辇
貿 – 贸	緬 – 缅	畝 – 亩	攆 – 撵
ㄇㄛ	麵 – 面	鉬 – 钼	ㄋㄧㄤ
麼 – 么	ㄇㄧㄠ	ㄋ	釀 – 酿
ㄇㄟ	鶓 – 鹋	ㄋㄚ	ㄋㄧㄠ
黴 – 霉	緲 – 缈	鎿 – 镎	鳥 – 鸟
鎇 – 镅	繆 – 缪	鈉 – 钠	蔦 – 茑
鶥 – 鹛	廟 – 庙	納 – 纳	裊 – 袅
鎂 – 镁	ㄇㄧㄝ	ㄋㄢ	ㄋㄧㄝ
ㄇㄣ	滅 – 灭	難 – 难	聶 – 聂
門 – 门	蠛 – 蔑	ㄋㄤ	顳 – 颞
捫 – 扪	ㄇㄧㄣ	饢 – 馕	囁 – 嗫
鍆 – 钔	緡 – 缗	ㄋㄠ	躡 – 蹑
懣 – 懑	閔 – 闵	撓 – 挠	鑷 – 镊
悶 – 闷	憫 – 悯	蟯 – 蛲	嚙 – 啮
燜 – 焖	閩 – 闽	鐃 – 铙	鎳 – 镍
們 – 们	黽 – 黾	惱 – 恼	ㄋㄧㄥ
ㄇㄥ	鰵 – 鳘	腦 – 脑	寧 – 宁
矇、濛、懞 – 蒙	ㄇㄧㄥ	鬧 – 闹	檸 – 柠
	鳴 – 鸣	ㄋㄜ	嚀 – 咛

獰 – 狞
聹 – 聍
擰 – 拧
濘 – 泞

ㄋㄧㄡ

鈕 – 钮
紐 – 纽

ㄋㄨㄥ

農 – 农
濃 – 浓
儂 – 侬
膿 – 脓
噥 – 哝

ㄋㄨ

駑 – 驽

ㄋㄩ

鈪 – 钕

ㄋㄩㄝ

瘧 – 疟

ㄋㄨㄛ

儺 – 傩
諾 – 诺
鍩 – 锘

ㄛ

ㄡ

區 – 区
謳 – 讴
甌 – 瓯
鷗 – 鸥
毆 – 殴
歐 – 欧

嘔 – 呕
漚 – 沤
慪 – 怄

ㄆ

ㄆㄢ

蹣 – 蹒
盤 – 盘

ㄆㄤ

鰟 – 鳑
龐 – 庞

ㄆㄟ

賠 – 赔
錇 – 锫
轡 – 辔

ㄆㄣ

噴 – 喷

ㄆㄥ

鵬 – 鹏

ㄆㄧ

紕 – 纰
羆 – 罴
鮍 – 鲏
鈹 – 铍
闢 – 辟
鸊 – 䴙

ㄆㄧㄢ

騈 – 骈
諞 – 谝
騙 – 骗

ㄆㄧㄠ

飄 – 飘

縹 – 缥
驃 – 骠

ㄆㄧㄣ

嬪 – 嫔
頻 – 频
顰 – 颦
貧 – 贫

ㄆㄧㄥ

評 – 评
蘋 – 苹
鮃 – 鲆
憑 – 凭

ㄆㄛ

鈸 – 钋
頗 – 颇
潑 – 泼
鏺 – 铍
鉕 – 钷

ㄆㄨ

鋪 – 铺
撲 – 扑
僕 – 仆
鏷 – 镤
譜 – 谱
鐠 – 镨
樸 – 朴

ㄑ

ㄑㄧ

緝 – 缉
榿 – 桤
齊 – 齐

蠐 – 蛴
臍 – 脐
騎 – 骑
騏 – 骐
鰭 – 鳍
頎 – 颀
蘄 – 蕲
啓 – 启
綺 – 绮
豈 – 岂
磧 – 碛
氣 – 气
訖 – 讫
薺 – 荠

ㄑㄧㄢ

騫 – 骞
謙 – 谦
慳 – 悭
牽 – 牵
僉 – 佥
簽、籤 – 签
韆 – 千
遷 – 迁
釺 – 钎
鉛 – 铅
鵮 – 鹐
蕁 – 荨
鉗 – 钳
錢 – 钱
鈐 – 钤
淺 – 浅

譴 – 谴	蕎 – 荞	瓊 – 琼	確 – 确
繾 – 缱	譙 – 谯	縈 – 茕	闋 – 阕
塹 – 堑	殼 – 壳	**ㄑㄧㄡ**	**ㄖ**
槧 – 椠	竅 – 窍	鞦 – 秋	**ㄖㄤ**
縴 – 纤	誚 – 诮	鶖 – 鹙	讓 – 让
ㄑㄧㄤ	**ㄑㄧㄝ**	鰍 – 鳅	**ㄖㄠ**
瑲 – 玱	鍥 – 锲	鰌 – 鳅	橈 – 桡
槍 – 枪	愜 – 惬	甃 – 甃	蕘 – 荛
鏘 – 锵	篋 – 箧	**ㄑㄩ**	饒 – 饶
墻 – 墙	竊 – 窃	麯 – 曲	嬈 – 娆
蘠 – 蔷	**ㄑㄧㄣ**	區 – 区	擾 – 扰
檣 – 樯	親 – 亲	驅 – 驱	繞 – 绕
嬙 – 嫱	欽 – 钦	嶇 – 岖	**ㄖㄜ**
鏹 – 锖	歆 – 嵚	軀 – 躯	熱 – 热
羥 – 羟	駸 – 骎	詘 – 诎	**ㄖㄣ**
搶 – 抢	寢 – 寝	趨 – 趋	認 – 认
熗 – 炝	鋟 – 锓	鴝 – 鸲	餁 – 饪
戧 – 戗	撳 – 揿	鼩 – 鼩	紝 – 纴
蹌 – 跄	**ㄑㄧㄥ**	覷 – 觑	軔 – 轫
嗆 – 呛	鯖 – 鲭	闃 – 阒	紉 – 纫
ㄑㄧㄠ	輕 – 轻	**ㄑㄩㄢ**	韌 – 韧
磽 – 硗	氫 – 氢	權 – 权	**ㄖㄨㄥ**
蹺 – 跷	傾 – 倾	顴 – 颧	榮 – 荣
鍬 – 锹	賄 – 赗	銓 – 铨	蠑 – 蝾
繰 – 缲	請 – 请	詮 – 诠	嶸 – 嵘
翹 – 翘	頃 – 顷	綣 – 绻	絨 – 绒
喬 – 乔	廎 – 庼	勸 – 劝	**ㄖㄨ**
橋 – 桥	慶 – 庆	**ㄑㄩㄝ**	銣 – 铷
礄 – 硚	**ㄑㄩㄥ**	愨 – 悫	顬 – 颥
僑 – 侨	窮 – 穷	鵲 – 鹊	縟 – 缛
轎 – 轿	藭 – 劳	闕 – 阙	

ㄖㄨㄢ	ㄕㄚ	捨 – 舍	獅 – 狮
軟 – 软	鯊 – 鲨	設 – 设	鳾 – 鸤
ㄖㄨㄟ	紗 – 纱	灄 – 滠	實 – 实
銳 – 锐	殺 – 杀	懾 – 慑	塒 – 埘
ㄖㄨㄣ	鎩 – 铩	攝 – 摄	鰣 – 鲥
閏 – 闰	ㄕㄞ	厙 – 库	識 – 识
潤 – 润	篩 – 筛	ㄕㄟ	時 – 时
ㄙ	曬 – 晒	誰 – 谁	蝕 – 蚀
ㄙㄚ	ㄕㄢ	ㄕㄣ	駛 – 驶
灑 – 洒	釤 – 钐	紳 – 绅	鈰 – 铈
颯 – 飒	陝 – 陕	參 – 参	視 – 视
薩 – 萨	閃 – 闪	糝 – 糁	諡 – 谥
ㄙㄞ	鐥 – 镨	審 – 审	試 – 试
鰓 – 鳃	鱔 – 鳝	譖 – 谮	軾 – 轼
賽 – 赛	繕 – 缮	嬸 – 婶	勢 – 势
ㄙㄢ	撣 – 掸	瀋 – 沈	蒔 – 莳
毿 – 毵	騸 – 骟	諗 – 谂	貰 – 贳
饊 – 馓	鍋 – 镐	腎 – 肾	釋 – 释
傘 – 伞	禪 – 禅	滲 – 渗	飾 – 饰
ㄙㄤ	訕 – 讪	瘆 – 瘆	適 – 适
喪 – 丧	贍 – 赡	ㄕㄥ	ㄕㄡ
纇 – 颡	ㄕㄤ	聲 – 声	獸 – 兽
ㄙㄠ	殤 – 殇	澠 – 渑	壽 – 寿
騷 – 骚	觴 – 觞	繩 – 绳	綬 – 绶
繅 – 缫	傷 – 伤	勝 – 胜	ㄕㄨ
掃 – 扫	賞 – 赏	聖 – 圣	樞 – 枢
ㄙㄜ	ㄕㄠ	ㄕ	攄 – 摅
澀 – 涩	燒 – 烧	濕 – 湿	輸 – 输
嗇 – 啬	紹 – 绍	詩 – 诗	紓 – 纾
穡 – 穑	ㄕㄜ	師 – 师	書 – 书
鈰 – 铯	賒 – 赊	獅 – 浉	贖 – 赎

屬 – 属　　　飼 – 饲　　　損 – 损　　　鉭 – 钽
數 – 数　　　　ㄙㄨㄥ　　　　ㄙㄨㄛ　　　嘆 – 叹
樹 – 树　　　鬆 – 松　　　縮 – 缩　　　　ㄊㄤ
術 – 术　　　慫 – 怂　　　璅 – 琐　　　鏜 – 镗
豎 – 竖　　　聳 – 耸　　　嗩 – 唢　　　湯 – 汤
　ㄕㄨㄞ　　　摐 – 㧽　　　鎖 – 锁　　　儻 – 傥
帥 – 帅　　　訟 – 讼　　　　ㄊ　　　　鏜 – 镋
　ㄕㄨㄢ　　　頌 – 颂　　　　ㄊㄚ　　　燙 – 烫
閂 – 闩　　　誦 – 诵　　　鉈 – 铊　　　　ㄊㄠ
　ㄕㄨㄤ　　　　ㄙㄡ　　　鰨 – 鳎　　　濤 – 涛
雙 – 双　　　餿 – 馊　　　獺 – 獭　　　韜 – 韬
瀧 – 泷　　　鎪 – 锼　　　澾 – 汏　　　縧 – 绦
　ㄕㄨㄟ　　　颼 – 飕　　　撻 – 挞　　　燾 – 焘
誰 – 谁　　　藪 – 薮　　　闥 – 闼　　　討 – 讨
　ㄕㄨㄣ　　　擻 – 擞　　　　ㄊㄞ　　　　ㄊㄜ
順 – 顺　　　　ㄙㄨ　　　臺、檯、颱 –　鋱 – 铽
　ㄕㄨㄛ　　　蘇、嚕 – 苏　　　台　　　　ㄊㄥ
說 – 说　　　穌 – 稣　　　駘 – 骀　　　謄 – 誊
碩 – 硕　　　謖 – 谡　　　鮐 – 鲐　　　騰 – 腾
爍 – 烁　　　訴 – 诉　　　態 – 态　　　縢 – 縢
鑠 – 铄　　　肅 – 肃　　　鈦 – 钛　　　　ㄊㄧ
　ㄙ　　　　　ㄙㄨㄟ　　　　ㄊㄢ　　　銻 – 锑
鍶 – 锶　　　雖 – 虽　　　灘 – 滩　　　鷈 – 鹏
颸 – 飔　　　隨 – 随　　　癱 – 瘫　　　鵜 – 鹈
釃 – 酾　　　綏 – 绥　　　攤 – 摊　　　綈 – 绨
緦 – 缌　　　歲 – 岁　　　貪 – 贪　　　緹 – 缇
絲 – 丝　　　誶 – 谇　　　談 – 谈　　　題 – 题
嘶 – 嘶　　　　ㄙㄨㄣ　　　壇、罈 – 坛　　體 – 体
鷥 – 鸶　　　孫 – 孙　　　譚 – 谭　　　　ㄊㄧㄢ
螄 – 蛳　　　蓀 – 荪　　　曇 – 昙　　　闐 – 阗
駟 – 驷　　　猻 – 狲　　　彈 – 弹　　　　ㄊㄧㄠ

條 – 条	飩 – 饨	韋 – 韦	齷 – 龌
鰷 – 鲦	**ㄊㄨㄛ**	違 – 违	**ㄨ**
齠 – 龆	飥 – 饦	圍 – 围	誣 – 诬
調 – 调	駝 – 驼	潿 – 涠	烏 – 乌
糶 – 粜	鴕 – 鸵	幃 – 帏	嗚 – 呜
ㄊㄧㄝ	馱 – 驮	闈 – 闱	鎢 – 钨
貼 – 贴	鼉 – 鼍	偽 – 伪	鄔 – 邬
鐵 – 铁	橢 – 椭	鮪 – 鲔	無 – 无
ㄊㄧㄥ	蘀 – 萚	諉 – 诿	蕪 – 芜
廳 – 厅	籜 – 箨	煒 – 炜	嫵 – 妩
烴 – 烃	**ㄨ**	瑋 – 玮	憮 – 怃
聽 – 听	**ㄨㄚ**	葦 – 苇	廡 – 庑
頲 – 颋	媧 – 娲	韙 – 韪	鵡 – 鹉
鋌 – 铤	窪 – 洼	偉 – 伟	塢 – 坞
ㄊㄨㄥ	襪 – 袜	緯 – 纬	務 – 务
銅 – 铜	**ㄨㄞ**	磑 – 硙	霧 – 雾
鮦 – 鲖	喎 – 㖞	謂 – 谓	鶩 – 鹜
統 – 统	**ㄨㄢ**	衛 – 卫	騖 – 骛
慟 – 恸	彎 – 弯	**ㄨㄣ**	誤 – 误
ㄊㄡ	灣 – 湾	鰛 – 鳁	**ㄒ**
頭 – 头	紈 – 纨	紋 – 纹	**ㄒㄧ**
ㄊㄨ	頑 – 顽	聞 – 闻	犧 – 牺
圖 – 图	綰 – 绾	閿 – 阌	餏 – 饻
塗 – 涂	萬 – 万	穩 – 稳	錫 – 锡
釷 – 钍	**ㄨㄤ**	問 – 问	襲 – 袭
ㄊㄨㄢ	網 – 网	**ㄨㄛ**	覡 – 觋
摶 – 抟	輞 – 辋	渦 – 涡	習 – 习
團、糰 – 团	**ㄨㄟ**	窩 – 窝	鰼 – 鳛
ㄊㄨㄟ	爲 – 为	萵 – 莴	璽 – 玺
頹 – 颓	維 – 维	蝸 – 蜗	銑 – 铣
ㄊㄨㄣ	濰 – 潍	撾 – 挝	係、繫 – 系

細 - 细
閱 - 阅
戲 - 戏
餼 - 饩

ㄒ丨ㄚ

蝦 - 虾
轄 - 辖
硤 - 硖
峽 - 峡
俠 - 侠
狹 - 狭
嚇 - 吓

ㄒ丨ㄢ

鮮 - 鲜
纖 - 纤
躚 - 跹
鍁 - 锨
薟 - 莶
賢 - 贤
鹹 - 咸
銜 - 衔
撏 - 挦
閑 - 闲
鷴 - 鹇
嫻 - 娴
癇 - 痫
蘚 - 藓
蜆 - 蚬
顯 - 显
險 - 险
獫 - 猃

銑 - 铣
獻 - 献
綫 - 线
現 - 现
莧 - 苋
峴 - 岘
縣 - 县
憲 - 宪
餡 - 馅

ㄒ丨ㄤ

驤 - 骧
鑲 - 镶
鄉 - 乡
薌 - 芗
緗 - 缃
詳 - 详
鯗 - 鲞
響 - 响
餉 - 饷
饗 - 飨
嚮 - 向
像 - 象
項 - 项

ㄒ丨ㄠ

驍 - 骁
嘵 - 哓
銷 - 销
綃 - 绡
囂 - 嚣
梟 - 枭
鴞 - 鸮

蕭 - 萧
瀟 - 潇
蠨 - 蟏
簫 - 箫
曉 - 晓
嘯 - 啸

ㄒ丨ㄝ

頡 - 颉
擷 - 撷
纈 - 缬
協 - 协
挾 - 挟
脅 - 胁
諧 - 谐
寫 - 写
褻 - 亵
瀉 - 泻
紲 - 绁
謝 - 谢

ㄒ丨ㄣ

鋅 - 锌
訢 - 䜣
釁 - 衅

ㄒ丨ㄥ

興 - 兴
滎 - 荥
鈃 - 钘
鉶 - 铏
陘 - 陉
餳 - 饧

ㄒㄩㄥ

訩 - 讻
詗 - 诇

ㄒ丨ㄡ

饈 - 馐
鵂 - 鸺
綉 - 绣
鏽 - 锈

ㄒㄩ

須、鬚 - 须
諝 - 谞
許 - 许
詡 - 诩
頊 - 顼
續 - 续
緒 - 绪

ㄒㄩㄢ

軒 - 轩
諼 - 谖
懸 - 悬
選 - 选
癬 - 癣
鏇 - 旋
鉉 - 铉
絢 - 绚

ㄒㄩㄝ

學 - 学
嶨 - 峃
鱈 - 鳕
謔 - 谑

ㄒㄩㄣ	嚴－严	ㄧㄠ	蟻－蚁
勛－勋	閻－阎	堯－尧	釔－钇
塤－埙	厴－厣	嶢－峣	誼－谊
馴－驯	鴈－鹰	謠－谣	瘞－瘗
詢－询	魘－魇	銚－铫	鎰－镒
尋－寻	儼－俨	輍－轺	縊－缢
潯－浔	巘－巇	瘍－疡	勩－勚
鱘－鲟	讞－谳	鷂－鹞	懌－怿
訓－训	讞－滟	鑰－钥	譯－译
訊－讯	厭－厌	藥－药	驛－驿
遜－逊	曆－餍	ㄧㄝ	嶧－峄
ㄧㄚ	贋－赝	爺－爷	繹－绎
壓－压	艷－艳	厴－厣	義－义
鴉－鸦	灔－滟	頁－页	議－议
鴨－鸭	讞－谳	燁－烨	軼－轶
釾－铘	硯－砚	暉－晔	藝－艺
啞－哑	覎－觃	業－业	囈－呓
氫－氩	釅－酽	鄴－邺	億－亿
亞－亚	驗－验	葉－叶	憶－忆
埡－垭	ㄧㄤ	謁－谒	詣－诣
掗－挜	鴦－鸯	ㄧ	鐿－镱
婭－娅	瘍－疡	鈥－铱	ㄧㄣ
訝－讶	煬－炀	醫－医	銦－铟
軋－轧	楊－杨	鷖－鹥	陰－阴
ㄧㄢ	揚－扬	禕－祎	蔭－荫
閼－阏	暘－旸	頤－颐	齦－龈
閹－阉	錫－钖	遺－遗	銀－银
懨－恹	陽－阳	儀－仪	飲－饮
顔－颜	癢－痒	詒－诒	隱－隐
鹽－盐	養－养	貽－贻	癮－瘾
	樣－样	飴－饴	廕－荫

ㄧㄥ	顒 – 颙	馭 – 驭	樂 – 乐
應 – 应	踴 – 踊	闔 – 阈	鑰 – 钥
鷹 – 鹰	ㄧㄡ	嫗 – 妪	ㄩㄣ
鶯 – 莺	憂 – 忧	鬱 – 郁	雲 – 云
罌 – 罂	優 – 优	諭 – 谕	蕓 – 芸
嬰 – 婴	魷 – 鱿	鵒 – 鹆	紜 – 纭
瓔 – 璎	猶 – 犹	飫 – 饫	澐 – 沄
櫻 – 樱	蕕 – 莸	獄 – 狱	鄖 – 郧
攖 – 撄	鈾 – 铀	預 – 预	殞 – 殒
嚶 – 嘤	郵 – 邮	澦 – 滪	隕 – 陨
鸚 – 鹦	銪 – 铕	蕷 – 蓣	惲 – 恽
纓 – 缨	誘 – 诱	鷸 – 鹬	暈 – 晕
熒 – 荧	ㄩ	ㄩㄢ	鄆 – 郓
瑩 – 莹	紆 – 纡	淵 – 渊	運 – 运
塋 – 茔	輿 – 舆	鳶 – 鸢	醞 – 酝
螢 – 萤	歟 – 欤	鴛 – 鸳	韞 – 韫
縈 – 萦	餘 – 余	黿 – 鼋	緼 – 缊
營 – 营	覦 – 觎	園 – 园	蘊 – 蕴
贏 – 赢	諛 – 谀	轅 – 辕	ㄗ
蠅 – 蝇	魚 – 鱼	員 – 员	ㄗㄚ
癭 – 瘿	漁 – 渔	圓 – 圆	臢 – 臜
穎 – 颖	歟 – 歟	緣 – 缘	雜 – 杂
穎 – 颖	與 – 与	橼 – 橼	ㄗㄞ
ㄛ	語 – 语	遠 – 远	載 – 载
喲 – 哟	齬 – 龉	願 – 愿	ㄗㄢ
ㄩㄥ	傴 – 伛	ㄩㄝ	趲 – 趱
癰 – 痈	嶼 – 屿	約 – 约	攢 – 攒
擁 – 拥	譽 – 誉	噦 – 哕	鏨 – 錾
傭 – 佣	鈺 – 钰	閱 – 阅	暫 – 暂
鏞 – 镛	籲 – 吁	鉞 – 钺	贊 – 赞
鱅 – 鳙	禦 – 御	躍 – 跃	瓚 – 瓒

ㄗㄤ	鮓 – 鲊	謫 – 谪	幀 – 帧
臢 – 赃	詐 – 诈	轍 – 辙	諍 – 诤
臟、髒 – 脏	**ㄓㄞ**	蟄 – 蛰	閘 – 闸
馸 – 驵	齋 – 斋	輒 – 辄	**ㄓ**
ㄗㄠ	債 – 债	讋 – 詟	隻、祇 – 只
鑿 – 凿	**ㄓㄢ**	摺 – 折	織 – 织
棗 – 枣	鸇 – 鹯	鍺 – 锗	職 – 职
竈 – 灶	鱣 – 鳣	這 – 这	躑 – 踯
ㄗㄜ	氈 – 毡	鷓 – 鹧	執 – 执
責 – 责	覘 – 觇	**ㄓㄣ**	縶 – 絷
嘖 – 啧	譫 – 谵	針 – 针	紙 – 纸
幘 – 帻	斬 – 斩	貞 – 贞	摯 – 挚
簀 – 箦	嶄 – 崭	湞 – 浈	贄 – 贽
則 – 则	盞 – 盏	禎 – 祯	鷙 – 鸷
鰂 – 鲗	輾 – 辗	楨 – 桢	擲 – 掷
澤 – 泽	綻 – 绽	偵 – 侦	滯 – 滞
擇 – 择	顫 – 颤	縝 – 缜	櫛 – 栉
ㄗㄟ	棧 – 栈	診 – 诊	輊 – 轾
賊 – 贼	戰 – 战	軫 – 轸	緻 – 致
ㄗㄣ	**ㄓㄤ**	鴆 – 鸩	幟 – 帜
譖 – 潛	張 – 张	賑 – 赈	製 – 制
ㄗㄥ	長 – 长	鎮 – 镇	質 – 质
繒 – 缯	漲 – 涨	紖 – 纼	躓 – 踬
贈 – 赠	帳 – 帐	陣 – 阵	鑕 – 锧
鋥 – 锃	賬 – 账	**ㄓㄥ**	騭 – 骘
ㄓㄚ	脹 – 胀	鉦 – 钲	**ㄓㄨㄥ**
鍘 – 铡	**ㄓㄠ**	徵 – 征	終 – 终
閘 – 闸	釗 – 钊	錚 – 铮	鐘、鍾 – 钟
軋 – 轧	趙 – 赵	癥 – 症	種 – 种
餷 – 馇	詔 – 诏	鄭 – 郑	腫 – 肿
	ㄓㄜ	證 – 证	衆 – 众

ㄓㄡ

謅 – 诌
賙 – 赒
鵃 – 鸼
軸 – 轴
紂 – 纣
葤 – 荮
驟 – 骤
皺 – 皱
縐 – 绉
惆 – 怞
儔 – 俦
晝 – 昼

ㄓㄨ

諸 – 诸
櫧 – 槠
硃 – 朱
誅 – 诛
銖 – 铢
燭 – 烛
囑 – 嘱
貯 – 贮
駐 – 驻
鑄 – 铸

築 – 筑

ㄓㄨㄚ

撾 – 挝

ㄓㄨㄢ

專 – 专
磚 – 砖
膞 – 膞
顓 – 颛
轉 – 转
囀 – 啭
賺 – 赚
傳 – 传
饌 – 馔

ㄓㄨㄤ

妝 – 妆
裝 – 装
莊 – 庄
樁 – 桩
戇 – 戆
壯 – 壮
狀 – 状

ㄓㄨㄟ

騅 – 骓

錐 – 锥
贅 – 赘
縋 – 缒
綴 – 缀
墜 – 坠

ㄓㄨㄣ

諄 – 谆
準 – 准

ㄓㄨㄛ

鐯 – 锗
濁 – 浊
諑 – 诼
鐲 – 镯

ㄗ

諮 – 谘
資 – 资
鎡 – 镃
齜 – 龇
輜 – 辎
錙 – 锱
緇 – 缁
鯔 – 鲻
漬 – 渍

ㄗㄨㄥ

綜 – 综
樅 – 枞
總 – 总
縱 – 纵

ㄗㄡ

諏 – 诹
鯫 – 鲰
騶 – 驺
鄒 – 邹

ㄗㄨ

鏃 – 镞
詛 – 诅
組 – 组

ㄗㄨㄢ

鑽 – 钻
躦 – 躜
纘 – 缵
賺 – 赚

ㄗㄨㄣ

鱒 – 鳟

ㄗㄨㄛ

鑿 – 凿

Strokes Index
筆劃索引

財 – 财
覎 – 觃
閃 – 闪
唄 – 呗
員 – 员
豈 – 岂
峽 – 峡
峴 – 岘
剛 – 刚
剮 – 剐

【丿】

氣 – 气
郵 – 邮
倀 – 伥
倆 – 俩
條 – 条
們 – 们
個 – 个
倫 – 伦
隻 – 只
島 – 岛
烏 – 乌
師 – 师
徑 – 径
釘 – 钉
針 – 针
釗 – 钊
釙 – 钋
釕 – 钌
殺 – 杀
倉 – 仓

脈 – 脉
飢 – 饥
脅 – 胁
狹 – 狭
狽 – 狈
芻 – 刍

【丶】

訐 – 讦
訌 – 讧
討 – 讨
訕 – 讪
訖 – 讫
訓 – 训
這 – 这
訊 – 讯
記 – 记
凍 – 冻
畝 – 亩
庫 – 库
浹 – 浃
涇 – 泾

【一】

書 – 书
陸 – 陆
陳 – 陈
孫 – 孙
陰 – 阴
務 – 务
紜 – 纭
純 – 纯
紕 – 纰

紗 – 纱
納 – 纳
紝 – 纴
紛 – 纷
紙 – 纸
紋 – 纹
紡 – 纺
紐 – 纠
紐 – 纽
紓 – 纾

11 劃

【一】

責 – 责
現 – 现
匭 – 匦
規 – 规
殼 – 壳
埡 – 垭
掛 – 挂
掗 – 挜
捨 – 舍
捫 – 扪
摑 – 掴
堝 – 埚
頂 – 顶
掄 – 抡
執 – 执
捲 – 卷
掃 – 扫
堊 – 垩

萊 – 莱
萵 – 莴
剳 – 札
乾 – 干
梘 – 枧
紮 – 扎
軛 – 轭
斬 – 斩
軟 – 软
專 – 专
區 – 区
堅 – 坚
脣 – 唇
帶 – 带
厠 – 厕
硃 – 朱
麥 – 麦
頃 – 顷

【丨】

鹵 – 卤
處 – 处
敗 – 败
販 – 贩
貶 – 贬
啞 – 哑
閉 – 闭
問 – 问
婁 – 娄
唄 – 唡
異 – 异
國 – 国

喎 – 喎	覓 – 觅	將 – 将	堯 – 尧
帳 – 帐	飥 – 饦	晝 – 昼	揀 – 拣
崬 – 崬	貧 – 贫	張 – 张	馭 – 驭
崍 – 崃	脛 – 胫	階 – 阶	項 – 项
崑 – 昆	週 – 周	陽 – 阳	貢 – 贡
崏 – 昆	魚 – 鱼	隊 – 队	場 – 场
崗 – 岗	【丶】	婭 – 娅	揚 – 扬
圇 – 囵	詎 – 讵	媧 – 娲	塊 – 块
過 – 过	訝 – 讶	婦 – 妇	達 – 达
【丿】	訥 – 讷	習 – 习	報 – 报
氫 – 氢	許 – 许	參 – 参	揮 – 挥
勛 – 动	訛 – 讹	紺 – 绀	壺 – 壶
偵 – 侦	訴 – 诉	紲 – 绁	惡 – 恶
側 – 侧	詡 – 诇	紱 – 绂	葉 – 叶
貨 – 货	訟 – 讼	組 – 组	貫 – 贯
進 – 进	設 – 设	紳 – 绅	萬 – 万
梟 – 枭	訪 – 访	紬 – 䌷	葷 – 荤
鳥 – 鸟	訣 – 诀	細 – 细	喪 – 丧
偉 – 伟	產 – 产	終 – 终	葦 – 苇
徠 – 徕	牽 – 牵	絆 – 绊	葒 – 荭
術 – 术	烴 – 烃	紼 – 绋	葤 – 荮
從 – 从	淶 – 涞	絀 – 绌	棖 – 枨
釷 – 钍	淺 – 浅	紹 – 绍	棟 – 栋
釺 – 钎	渦 – 涡	給 – 给	棲 – 栖
釧 – 钏	淪 – 沦	貫 – 贯	棧 – 栈
釤 – 钐	淚 – 泪	鄉 – 乡	椆 – 枏
釣 – 钓	悵 – 怅		極 – 极
釩 – 钒	鄆 – 郓	**12 劃**	軲 – 轱
釹 – 钕	啓 – 启	【一】	軻 – 轲
釵 – 钗	視 – 视	貳 – 贰	軸 – 轴
貪 – 贪	【一】	頂 – 顶	軼 – 轶

軤 – 轷
軫 – 轸
軺 – 轺
畫 – 画
腎 – 肾
棗 – 枣
硨 – 砗
硤 – 硖
硯 – 砚
殘 – 残
雲 – 云

【丨】

覘 – 觇
睏 – 困
貼 – 贴
貺 – 贶
貯 – 贮
貽 – 贻
閏 – 闰
開 – 开
閑 – 闲
間 – 间
閔 – 闵
悶 – 闷
貴 – 贵
鄖 – 郧
勛 – 勋
單 – 单
喲 – 哟
買 – 买
剴 – 剀
凱 – 凯
幀 – 帧
嵐 – 岚
幃 – 帏
圍 – 围

【丿】

無 – 无
氬 – 氩
喬 – 乔
筍 – 笋
筆 – 笔
備 – 备
貸 – 贷
順 – 顺
傖 – 伧
傑 – 杰
㑳 – 㑇
傢 – 家
鄔 – 邬
衆 – 众
復 – 复
須 – 须
鈃 – 钘
鈣 – 钙
鈈 – 钚
鈦 – 钛
鉅 – 巨
釾 – 𬬻
鈍 – 钝
鈔 – 钞
鈉 – 钠
鈐 – 钤
欽 – 钦
鈞 – 钧
鈎 – 钩
鈧 – 钪
鈁 – 钫
鈥 – 钬
鈄 – 钭
鈕 – 钮
鈀 – 钯
傘 – 伞
爺 – 爷
創 – 创
飩 – 饨
飪 – 饪
飫 – 饫
飭 – 饬
飯 – 饭
飲 – 饮
爲 – 为
脹 – 胀
腖 – 胨
腡 – 脶
勝 – 胜
猶 – 犹
貿 – 贸
鄒 – 邹

【丶】

詁 – 诂
訶 – 诃
評 – 评
詛 – 诅
詗 – 诇
詐 – 诈
訴 – 诉
診 – 诊
詆 – 诋
註 – 注
詞 – 词
詘 – 诎
詔 – 诏
詒 – 诒
馮 – 冯
痙 – 痉
勞 – 劳
湞 – 浈
測 – 测
湯 – 汤
淵 – 渊
渢 – 沨
渾 – 浑
湧 – 涌
愜 – 惬
惻 – 恻
惲 – 恽
惱 – 恼
運 – 运
補 – 补
禍 – 祸

【乛】

尋 – 寻
費 – 费

違 – 违	塒 – 埘	賈 – 贾	嗆 – 呛
靭 – 韧	填 – 填	匯 – 汇	圓 – 圆
隕 – 陨	損 – 损	電 – 电	骯 – 肮
賀 – 贺	遠 – 远	頓 – 顿	**【丿】**
發 – 发	塏 – 垲	盞 – 盏	筥 – 筥
綁 – 绑	勢 – 势	**【丨】**	節 – 节
絨 – 绒	搶 – 抢	歲 – 岁	與 – 与
結 – 结	搗 – 捣	虜 – 虏	債 – 债
綺 – 绮	塢 – 坞	業 – 业	僅 – 仅
经 – 经	壺 – 壶	當 – 当	傳 – 传
絎 – 绗	聖 – 圣	睞 – 睐	傴 – 伛
給 – 给	蓋 – 盖	賊 – 贼	傾 – 倾
絢 – 绚	蓮 – 莲	賄 – 贿	僂 – 偻
絳 – 绛	蒔 – 莳	賂 – 赂	賃 – 赁
絡 – 络	蓽 – 荜	賅 – 赅	傷 – 伤
絞 – 绞	夢 – 梦	嗎 – 吗	傭 – 佣
統 – 统	蒼 – 苍	嘩 – 哗	裊 – 袅
絕 – 绝	蓆 – 席	嗊 – 唝	頎 – 颀
絲 – 丝	幹 – 干	暘 – 旸	鈺 – 钰
幾 – 几	蓀 – 荪	闈 – 闱	鉦 – 钲
13 劃	蔭 – 荫	黿 – 鼋	鉗 – 钳
【一】	蒓 – 莼	暈 – 晕	鈷 – 钴
項 – 项	楨 – 桢	號 – 号	鉢 – 钵
瑃 – 珲	楊 – 杨	園 – 园	鉅 – 钜
瑋 – 玮	嗇 – 啬	跡 – 迹	鈳 – 钶
頑 – 顽	楓 – 枫	蛺 – 蛱	鈸 – 钹
載 – 载	軾 – 轼	蜆 – 蚬	鉞 – 钺
馱 – 驮	輊 – 轾	農 – 农	鉬 – 钼
馴 – 驯	輅 – 辂	嗩 – 唢	鉏 – 钼
馳 – 驰	較 – 较	嗶 – 哔	鉀 – 钾
	竪 – 竖	鳴 – 鸣	鈾 – 铀

鈿－钿	誆－诓	煬－炀	絹－绢
鉑－铂	誅－诔	塋－茔	綉－绣
鈴－铃	試－试	熒－荧	綏－绥
鉛－铅	註－诖	煒－炜	綈－绨
鉚－铆	詩－诗	遞－递	彙－汇
鉰－铈	詰－诘	溝－沟	
鉉－铉	誇－夸	漣－涟	**14 劃**
鉈－铊	詼－诙	滅－灭	
鉍－铋	誠－诚	溳－涢	【一】
鈮－铌	誅－诛	滌－涤	瑪－玛
鈹－铍	話－话	澌－澌	璉－琏
僉－佥	誕－诞	塗－涂	瑣－琐
會－会	詬－诟	滄－沧	瑲－玱
亂－乱	詮－诠	愷－恺	駁－驳
愛－爱	詭－诡	愾－忾	搏－抟
飾－饰	詢－询	愴－怆	摳－抠
飽－饱	詣－诣	惘－怡	趙－赵
飼－饲	諍－净	窩－窝	趕－赶
蝕－蚀	該－该	禎－祯	摟－搂
飴－饴	詳－详	褘－祎	摑－掴
頌－颂	詫－诧		臺－台
頌－颂	詡－诩	【一】	摢－抟
腸－肠	裏－里	肅－肃	墊－垫
腫－肿	準－准	裝－装	壽－寿
腦－脑	頏－颃	遜－逊	摺－折
魝－魝	資－资	際－际	摻－掺
猧－犸	棄－弃	媽－妈	摜－掼
鳩－鸠	羥－羟	預－预	勘－勘
獅－狮	義－义	綆－绠	蔓－蔓
猻－狲	煉－炼	經－经	蔫－蔫
【丶】	煩－烦	綃－绡	蓯－苁
		緆－绲	萄－卜

蔴 – 麻　　　　　嘖 – 啧　　　　　圖 – 图　　　　　銚 – 铫

蔣 – 蒋　　　　　曄 – 晔　　　　　【丿】　　　　　銘 – 铭

鄉 – 乡　　　　　夥 – 伙　　　　　製　制　　　　　鉻 – 铬

構 – 构　　　　　賑 – 赈　　　　　稭 – 秸　　　　　錚 – 铮

樺 – 桦　　　　　賒 – 赊　　　　　種 – 种　　　　　鉋 – 铇

橙 – 桤　　　　　嘆 – 叹　　　　　稱 – 称　　　　　鉸 – 铰

覡 – 觋　　　　　暢 – 畅　　　　　箋 – 笺　　　　　鉄 – 铱

槍 – 枪　　　　　嘜 – 唛　　　　　剳 – 札　　　　　銃 – 铳

輒 – 辄　　　　　閨 – 闺　　　　　僥 – 侥　　　　　銨 – 铵

輔 – 辅　　　　　聞 – 闻　　　　　債 – 债　　　　　銀 – 银

輕 – 轻　　　　　閧 – 哄　　　　　僕 – 仆　　　　　鉚 – 铆

塹 – 堑　　　　　閩 – 闽　　　　　僑 – 侨　　　　　餞 – 饯

匱 – 匮　　　　　閭 – 闾　　　　　僞 – 伪　　　　　餌 – 饵

監 – 监　　　　　閥 – 阀　　　　　催 – 雇　　　　　蝕 – 蚀

緊 – 紧　　　　　閣 – 合　　　　　衒 – 衔　　　　　餇 – 饷

厲 – 厉　　　　　閣 – 阁　　　　　鉚 – 铆　　　　　餄 – 饸

厭 – 厌　　　　　閘 – 闸　　　　　銬 – 铐　　　　　餎 – 饹

碩 – 硕　　　　　閡 – 阂　　　　　鉺 – 铑　　　　　餃 – 饺

碭 – 砀　　　　　嘔 – 呕　　　　　鉺 – 铒　　　　　鉷 – 铱

颮 – 飑　　　　　蝸 – 蜗　　　　　鏜 – 铛　　　　　餅 – 饼

盦 – 夜　　　　　團 – 团　　　　　銪 – 铕　　　　　領 – 领

爾 – 尔　　　　　嘍 – 喽　　　　　鋁 – 铝　　　　　鳳 – 凤

奪 – 夺　　　　　鄲 – 郸　　　　　銅 – 铜　　　　　颱 – 台

殞 – 殒　　　　　鳴 – 鸣　　　　　錦 – 锦　　　　　獄 – 狱

鳶 – 鸢　　　　　幘 – 帻　　　　　銦 – 铟　　　　　【丶】

甀 – 甃　　　　　嶄 – 崭　　　　　銖 – 铢　　　　　誠 – 诚

【丨】　　　　　嶇 – 岖　　　　　銑 – 铣　　　　　誣 – 诬

對 – 对　　　　　獃 – 呆　　　　　銩 – 铥　　　　　語 – 语

幣 – 币　　　　　罰 – 罚　　　　　鋌 – 铤　　　　　誚 – 诮

彆 – 别　　　　　嶁 – 嵝　　　　　銓 – 铨　　　　　誤 – 误

嘗 – 尝　　　　　幗 – 帼　　　　　鉿 – 铪　　　　　誥 – 诰

誘 – 诱	滯 – 滞	墜 – 坠	鬧 – 闹
誨 – 诲	滷 – 卤	嫗 – 妪	璕 – 琎
誆 – 诓	漊 – 溇	頗 – 颇	靚 – 靓
說 – 说	漁 – 渔	態 – 态	輦 – 辇
認 – 认	滸 – 浒	鄧 – 邓	髮 – 发
誦 – 诵	漣 – 涟	緒 – 绪	撓 – 挠
誒 – 诶	滬 – 沪	綾 – 绫	墳 – 坟
廣 – 广	漲 – 涨	綺 – 绮	撻 – 挞
麼 – 么	滲 – 渗	綫 – 线	駔 – 驵
廎 – 庼	慚 – 惭	緋 – 绯	駛 – 驶
瘖 – 疟	慪 – 怄	綽 – 绰	駒 – 驹
瘍 – 疡	慳 – 悭	緄 – 绲	駙 – 驸
瘋 – 疯	慟 – 恸	綱 – 纲	駒 – 驹
塵 – 尘	慘 – 惨	網 – 网	駐 – 驻
颯 – 飒	慣 – 惯	維 – 维	駝 – 驼
適 – 适	寬 – 宽	綿 – 绵	駘 – 骀
齊 – 齐	賓 – 宾	綸 – 纶	撲 – 扑
養 – 养	窪 – 洼	綬 – 绶	頡 – 颉
鄰 – 邻	寧 – 宁	綳 – 绷	撣 – 掸
鄭 – 郑	寢 – 寝	綢 – 绸	賣 – 卖
燁 – 烨	實 – 实	綹 – 绺	撫 – 抚
熗 – 炝	靸 – 靸	綣 – 绻	撟 – 挢
榮 – 荣	複 – 复	綜 – 综	撳 – 揿
熒 – 荧	**【一】**	綻 – 绽	熱 – 热
犖 – 荦	劃 – 划	綰 – 绾	鞏 – 巩
熒 – 荧	盡 – 尽	綠 – 绿	摯 – 挚
潰 – 溃	屢 – 屡	綴 – 缀	撈 – 捞
漢 – 汉	獎 – 奖	緇 – 缁	穀 – 谷
滿 – 满	墮 – 堕		慤 – 悫
漸 – 渐	隨 – 随	**15 劃**	撏 – 挦
漚 – 沤	靴 – 鞑	**【一】**	撥 – 拨

劊 – 刽
鄶 – 郐
猫 – 猫
餚 – 肴
餓 – 饿
餘 – 余
餒 – 馁
膊 – 胉
膕 – 腘
膠 – 胶
鋯 – 锆
魷 – 鱿
魯 – 鲁
魴 – 鲂
潁 – 颍
颳 – 刮
劉 – 刘
皺 – 皱

【丶】

請 – 请
諸 – 诸
諏 – 诹
諾 – 诺
諑 – 诼
誹 – 诽
課 – 课
諉 – 诿
諛 – 谀
誰 – 谁
論 – 论
諗 – 谂

調 – 调
諂 – 谄
諒 – 谅
諄 – 谆
諱 – 讳
談 – 谈
誼 – 谊
廟 – 庙
廠 – 厂
廡 – 庑
瘞 – 瘗
瘡 – 疮
賡 – 赓
慶 – 庆
廢 – 废
敵 – 敌
頦 – 颏
導 – 导
瑩 – 莹
潔 – 洁
澆 – 浇
澾 – 达
潤 – 润
澗 – 涧
潰 – 溃
潿 – 涠
濬 – 浚
潙 – 沩
澇 – 涝
潯 – 浔
潑 – 泼

憒 – 愦
憫 – 悯
憒 – 愦
慣 – 惯
憚 – 惮
憮 – 怃
憐 – 怜
寫 – 写
審 – 审
窮 – 穷
褳 – 裢
褲 – 裤
鳲 – 鸤

【一】

遲 – 迟
層 – 层
彈 – 弹
選 – 选
槳 – 桨
漿 – 浆
險 – 险
嬈 – 娆
嫻 – 娴
駕 – 驾
嬋 – 婵
嫵 – 妩
嬌 – 娇
嫣 – 妈
嫗 – 妪
駑 – 驽
輦 – 辇
氄 – 氄

緙 – 缂
緗 – 缃
練 – 练
緘 – 缄
緬 – 缅
緹 – 缇
緲 – 缈
緝 – 缉
縕 – 缊
緦 – 缌
緞 – 缎
緱 – 缑
縋 – 缒
緩 – 缓
締 – 缔
編 – 编
緡 – 缗
緯 – 纬
緣 – 缘

16 劃

【一】

璣 – 玑
墻 – 墙
駱 – 骆
駭 – 骇
駢 – 骈
擓 – 㧟
擄 – 掳
擋 – 挡
擇 – 择

楨 – 桢	磚 – 砖	踴 – 踊	鴕 – 鸵
撿 – 捡	磽 – 硗	螞 – 蚂	艙 – 舱
擔 – 担	歷 – 历	螄 – 蛳	錶 – 表
壇 – 坛	曆 – 历	噹 – 当	鍺 – 锗
擁 – 拥	奮 – 奋	罵 – 骂	錯 – 错
據 – 据	煩 – 烦	噥 – 哝	鍩 – 锘
薔 – 蔷	殪 – 殨	戰 – 战	錨 – 锚
薑 – 姜	殫 – 殚	噲 – 哙	錛 – 锛
薈 – 荟	頸 – 颈	鴦 – 鸯	錸 – 铼
薊 – 蓟	【丨】	嗳 – 嗳	錢 – 钱
薦 – 荐	閧 – 哄	嘯 – 啸	錁 – 锞
蕭 – 萧	頻 – 频	還 – 还	錁 – 锞
頤 – 颐	盧 – 卢	嶧 – 峄	錕 – 锟
鴣 – 鸪	曉 – 晓	嶼 – 屿	鍆 – 钔
薩 – 萨	瞞 – 瞒	【丿】	錫 – 锡
蕷 – 蓣	縣 – 县	積 – 积	錮 – 锢
橈 – 桡	嘔 – 呕	頹 – 颓	鋼 – 钢
樹 – 树	瞜 – 䁖	穆 – 穆	鍋 – 锅
樸 – 朴	賵 – 赗	篤 – 笃	錘 – 锤
橋 – 桥	鴨 – 鸭	築 – 筑	錐 – 锥
機 – 机	閾 – 阈	筆 – 笔	錦 – 锦
輳 – 辏	閹 – 阉	篩 – 筛	鍬 – 锹
輻 – 辐	閭 – 闾	舉 – 举	錇 – 锫
輯 – 辑	閶 – 阊	興 – 兴	錠 – 锭
輸 – 输	閽 – 阍	嶨 – 峃	鍵 – 键
賴 – 赖	閻 – 阎	學 – 学	錄 – 录
頭 – 头	閼 – 阏	儔 – 俦	鋸 – 锯
醃 – 腌	曇 – 昙	憊 – 惫	錳 – 锰
醜 – 丑	噸 – 吨	儕 – 侪	錙 – 锱
勵 – 励	鴉 – 鸦	儐 – 傧	覦 – 觎
磧 – 碛	噦 – 哕	盡 – 尽	墾 – 垦

餞 – 饯	諫 – 谏	縈 – 萦	繈 – 绺
餜 – 馃	諧 – 谐	燈 – 灯	繚 – 缭
餛 – 馄	謔 – 谑	濛 – 蒙	縞 – 缟
餡 – 馅	謁 – 谒	燙 – 烫	縭 – 缡
館 – 馆	謂 – 谓	澠 – 渑	縑 – 缣
頜 – 颌	諤 – 谔	濃 – 浓	縊 – 缢
鴿 – 鸽	諭 – 谕	澤 – 泽	
膩 – 腻	諼 – 谖	濁 – 浊	**17 劃**
鷗 – 鸥	諷 – 讽	澮 – 浍	
鮁 – 鲅	諮 – 谘	澱 – 淀	**【一】**
鮃 – 鲆	諳 – 谙	澠 – 澜	檁 – 檩
鮎 – 鲇	諺 – 谚	懞 – 蒙	環 – 环
鮓 – 鲊	諦 – 谛	懌 – 怿	贅 – 赘
穌 – 稣	謎 – 谜	憶 – 忆	璦 – 瑷
鮒 – 鲋	諢 – 诨	憲 – 宪	覯 – 觏
卿 – 卿	論 – 论	窺 – 窥	黿 – 鼋
鮑 – 鲍	諱 – 讳	寰 – 窭	幫 – 帮
鮍 – 鲏	謅 – 诌	寫 – 写	騁 – 骋
鮐 – 鲐	憑 – 凭	褸 – 褛	駸 – 骎
鴝 – 鸲	廒 – 庼	禪 – 禅	駿 – 呆
獲 – 获	瘦 – 瘘		駿 – 骏
穎 – 颖	瘮 – 瘆	**【一】**	趨 – 趋
獨 – 独	親 – 亲	隱 – 隐	擱 – 搁
獪 – 狯	辦 – 办	嬙 – 嫱	擬 – 拟
獫 – 猃	龍 – 龙	嬡 – 嫒	擴 – 扩
鴛 – 鸳	劑 – 剂	縉 – 缙	壙 – 圹
	燒 – 烧	縝 – 缜	擠 – 挤
【丶】	燜 – 焖	縛 – 缚	蟄 – 蛰
諜 – 谋	熾 – 炽	縟 – 缛	縶 – 絷
諶 – 谌	螢 – 萤	緻 – 致	擲 – 掷
諜 – 谍	營 – 营	縲 – 缧	擯 – 摈
謊 – 谎		縫 – 缝	擰 – 拧

轂 – 毂	尷 – 尴	嶸 – 嵘	鍐 – 锾
聲 – 声	騺 – 骘	嶽 – 岳	鑌 – 镔
藉 – 借	殮 – 殓	點 – 点	鍍 – 镀
聰 – 聪	【丨】	【丿】	鎂 – 镁
聯 – 联	齔 – 龀	矯 – 矫	鎇 – 镅
艱 – 艰	戲 – 戏	鴰 – 鸹	鋦 – 锔
藍 – 蓝	虧 – 亏	簀 – 箦	懇 – 恳
舊 – 旧	斃 – 毙	簍 – 篓	餿 – 馊
薺 – 荠	暸 – 了	輿 – 舆	餳 – 饧
藎 – 荩	顆 – 颗	欻 – 欻	餶 – 馉
韓 – 韩	購 – 购	鵂 – 鸺	餿 – 馊
隸 – 隶	賻 – 赙	鼂 – 鼋	斂 – 敛
檉 – 柽	嬰 – 婴	優 – 优	鴿 – 鸽
檣 – 樯	賺 – 赚	償 – 偿	膿 – 脓
檟 – 槚	嚇 – 吓	儲 – 储	臉 – 脸
檔 – 档	闌 – 阑	魍 – 魍	膾 – 脍
櫛 – 栉	闃 – 阒	鵃 – 鸼	膽 – 胆
檢 – 检	闆 – 板	禦 – 御	膳 – 誊
檜 – 桧	闊 – 阔	聳 – 耸	鮭 – 鲑
麯 – 曲	闈 – 闱	鴴 – 鸻	鮚 – 鲒
轅 – 辕	闋 – 阕	鍥 – 锲	鮪 – 鲔
轄 – 辖	曖 – 暧	鍇 – 锴	鮦 – 鲖
輾 – 辗	蹕 – 跸	鍘 – 铡	鮫 – 鲛
擊 – 击	蹌 – 跄	鍚 – 钖	鮮 – 鲜
臨 – 临	蟎 – 螨	鍶 – 锶	颶 – 飓
磽 – 硗	螻 – 蝼	鍔 – 锷	獷 – 犷
壓 – 压	蟈 – 蝈	鍤 – 锸	獰 – 狞
礄 – 硚	雖 – 虽	鐘 – 钟	【丶】
磯 – 矶	嚀 – 咛	鍛 – 锻	講 – 讲
鴯 – 鸸	覬 – 觊	鎪 – 锼	謨 – 谟
邇 – 迩	嶺 – 岭	鍬 – 锹	謖 – 谡

謝 – 谢	澀 – 泾	釐 – 厘	檻 – 槛
謠 – 谣	澀 – 涩	攒 – 攒	櫚 – 桐
謅 – 诌	濰 – 潍	鬆 – 松	檳 – 槟
謗 – 谤	懨 – 恹	翹 – 翘	檸 – 柠
謚 – 谥	賽 – 赛	擷 – 撷	鵓 – 鹁
謙 – 谦	襇 – 裥	擾 – 扰	轉 – 转
謐 – 谧	襖 – 褴	騏 – 骐	轆 – 辘
褻 – 亵	襖 – 袄	騎 – 骑	醫 – 医
氈 – 毡	禮 – 礼	騍 – 骒	礎 – 础
應 – 应	【一】	雛 – 雏	殯 – 殡
癘 – 疠	履 – 屦	攄 – 摅	霧 – 雾
療 – 疗	彌 – 弥	擻 – 擞	【丨】
癇 – 痫	嬪 – 嫔	蟄 – 冬	豐 – 丰
癉 – 瘅	績 – 绩	擺 – 摆	覷 – 觑
癆 – 痨	縹 – 缥	贅 – 赘	懟 – 怼
鷄 – 鸡	縷 – 缕	熹 – 焘	叢 – 丛
齋 – 斋	縵 – 缦	聶 – 聂	矇 – 蒙
羞 – 羞	繆 – 缧	職 – 聩	題 – 题
鼇 – 鳌	總 – 总	職 – 职	釐 – 赿
糞 – 粪	縱 – 纵	藝 – 艺	瞼 – 睑
糝 – 糁	縴 – 纤	覲 – 觐	闖 – 闯
燦 – 灿	縮 – 缩	鞦 – 秋	闔 – 阖
燭 – 烛	繆 – 缪	藪 – 薮	闐 – 阗
燴 – 烩	繅 – 缫	蠆 – 虿	闉 – 闾
鴻 – 鸿	嚮 – 向	繭 – 茧	闋 – 阕
濤 – 涛		藥 – 药	顋 – 颗
濫 – 滥	**18 劃**	薅 – 莠	曠 – 旷
濕 – 湿	【一】	賾 – 赜	蹟 – 迹
濟 – 济	檮 – 梼	蘊 – 蕴	蹣 – 蹒
濱 – 滨	閱 – 阅	檯 – 台	嚙 – 啮
濘 – 泞	瓊 – 琼	櫃 – 柜	壘 – 垒

蟯－蛲	鎦－镏	癤－疖	繕－缮
蠱－蛊	鎬－镐	雜－杂	繒－缯
蟬－蝉	鎊－镑	離－离	繡－绣
蟣－虮	鎰－镒	顏－颜	斷－断
鵑－鹃	鎵－镓	糧－粮	
嚕－噜	鎘－镉	燼－烬	**19 劃**
顓－颛	鴿－鸽	鵜－鹈	
【丿】	饃－馍	瀆－渎	**【一】**
鵠－鹄	餺－馎	蕙－蒽	鵡－鹉
鵝－鹅	餼－饩	瀘－泸	鵲－鹊
穫－获	餾－馏	鯊－鲨	鬍－胡
穡－穑	饊－馓	濺－溅	騙－骗
穢－秽	臍－脐	瀏－浏	騷－骚
簡－简	鯁－鲠	濼－泺	壢－坜
簣－篑	鯉－鲤	瀉－泻	壚－垆
簞－箪	鯀－鲧	瀋－沈	壞－坏
雙－双	鮸－鮸	竄－窜	攏－拢
軀－躯	鯽－鲫	竅－窍	攔－拦
邊－边	颺－飏	額－额	難－难
歸－归	颸－飔	禰－祢	鵲－鹊
鏵－铧	觴－觞	襠－裆	蘑－莤
鎮－镇	獵－猎	襝－裣	蘋－苹
鏈－链	雛－雏	燾－焘	蘆－芦
鎘－镉	臏－膑		鵪－鹌
鎖－锁	**【丶】**	**【一】**	蔄－蔄
鎧－铠	謹－谨	醬－酱	藭－茕
鐫－镌	謳－讴	韞－韫	蘄－蕲
鎳－镍	謾－谩	隴－陇	勸－劝
鎢－钨	謫－谪	嬙－嫱	蘇－苏
鍛－锬	謭－谫	繞－绕	藹－蔼
鏵－锋	謬－谬	繚－缭	龐－庞
		織－织	顛－颠

櫝 – 椟
櫟 – 栎
櫓 – 橹
櫧 – 槠
櫞 – 橼
轎 – 轿
鏨 – 錾
轍 – 辙
轔 – 辚
繫 – 系
鶇 – 鸫
麗 – 丽
厴 – 厣
礪 – 砺
礙 – 碍
礦 – 矿
贗 – 赝
願 – 愿
鵪 – 鹌
璽 – 玺
豶 – 豮

【丨】

贈 – 赠
闞 – 阚
關 – 关
嚦 – 呖
疇 – 畴
蹺 – 跷
蟶 – 蛏
蠅 – 蝇
蟻 – 蚁
嚴 – 严
獸 – 兽
嚨 – 咙
羆 – 罴
羅 – 罗

【丿】

氌 – 氇
犢 – 犊
贊 – 赞
穩 – 稳
簽 – 签
簾 – 帘
簫 – 箫
牘 – 牍
懲 – 惩
鐯 – 𫓹
鏗 – 铿
鏢 – 镖
鏜 – 镗
鏤 – 镂
鏝 – 镘
鏰 – 镚
鏞 – 镛
鏡 – 镜
鏟 – 铲
鏑 – 镝
鏃 – 镞
鏇 – 旋
鏘 – 锵
辭 – 辞
饉 – 馑
饅 – 馒
鵬 – 鹏
臘 – 腊
鯖 – 鲭
鯪 – 鲮
鯫 – 鲰
鯡 – 鲱
鯤 – 鲲
鯧 – 鲳
鯢 – 鲵
鯰 – 鲶
鯛 – 鲷
鯨 – 鲸
鯔 – 鲻
獺 – 獭
鵮 – 鹐
飀 – 飗

【丶】

譚 – 谭
譖 – 谮
譙 – 谯
識 – 识
譜 – 谱
證 – 证
譎 – 谲
譏 – 讥
鶉 – 鹑
廬 – 庐
癟 – 瘪
癡 – 痴
癢 – 痒
龐 – 庞
壟 – 垄
韻 – 韵
鶊 – 鹒
類 – 类
爍 – 烁
瀟 – 潇
瀨 – 濑
瀝 – 沥
瀕 – 濒
瀘 – 泸
瀧 – 泷
懶 – 懒
懷 – 怀
寵 – 宠
襪 – 袜
襤 – 褴

【乛】

韜 – 韬
騭 – 骘
騖 – 骛
顙 – 颡
繮 – 缰
繩 – 绳
繾 – 缱
繰 – 缲
繹 – 绎
繯 – 缳
繳 – 缴
繪 – 绘

20 劃

【一】
瓏 – 珑
鶩 – 骜
驊 – 骅
騮 – 骝
騶 – 驺
騸 – 骟
攖 – 撄
攔 – 拦
攙 – 搀
聹 – 聍
顢 – 颟
驀 – 蓦
蘭 – 兰
蘞 – 蔹
蘚 – 藓
鶘 – 鹕
飄 – 飘
櫪 – 枥
櫨 – 栌
欅 – 榉
礬 – 矾
麵 – 面
櫬 – 榇
櫳 – 栊
礫 – 砾
【丨】
鹹 – 咸
鹺 – 鹾
齟 – 龃
齡 – 龄
齣 – 出
齙 – 龅
齠 – 龆
獻 – 献
黨 – 党
懸 – 悬
鶪 – 䴗
罌 – 罂
贍 – 赡
闥 – 闼
闡 – 阐
鶡 – 鹖
嚨 – 咙
蠣 – 蛎
蠐 – 蛴
蠑 – 蝾
嚶 – 嘤
鶚 – 鹗
髏 – 髅
鶻 – 鹘
【丿】
犧 – 牺
鶖 – 鹙
籌 – 筹
籃 – 篮
譽 – 誉
覺 – 觉
嚳 – 喾
衊 – 蔑
艦 – 舰
鐃 – 铙
鐝 – 镢
鐐 – 镣
鏷 – 镤
鐦 – 锎
鐧 – 锏
鐓 – 镦
鐘 – 钟
鐥 – 𬭊
鐠 – 镨
鐒 – 铹
鎸 – 镌
鐲 – 镯
鐨 – 镄
鐙 – 镫
鏺 – 钹
釋 – 释
饒 – 饶
饊 – 馓
饋 – 馈
饌 – 馔
饑 – 饥
臚 – 胪
朧 – 胧
騰 – 腾
鰆 – 䲠
鰈 – 鲽
鰂 – 鲗
鰛 – 鳁
鰓 – 鳃
鰐 – 鳄
鰍 – 鳅
鰒 – 鳆
鰉 – 鳇
鰌 – 䲡
鯿 – 鳊
獼 – 猕
觸 – 触
【丶】
護 – 护
譴 – 谴
譯 – 译
譫 – 谵
議 – 议
癥 – 症
辮 – 辫
龑 – 䶮
競 – 竞
贏 – 赢
糲 – 粝
糰 – 团
鶿 – 鹚
爐 – 炉
瀾 – 澜
瀲 – 潋
瀰 – 弥
懺 – 忏
寶 – 宝
騫 – 骞
竇 – 窦
擺 – 摆

【一】

鷉－鹉
鷟－莺
纊－矿
繽－缤
繼－继
饗－飨
響－响

21 劃

【一】

糯－糯
瓔－璎
鰲－鳌
攝－摄
騾－骡
驅－驱
驃－骠
驄－骢
驂－骖
攄－抒
擻－擞
韃－鞑
轎－轿
歡－欢
權－权
樱－樱
欄－栏
轟－轰
覽－览
酈－郦

飆－飙
殲－歼

【丨】

齜－龇
齦－龈
齣－龀
贐－赆
囁－嗫
囈－呓
闢－辟
囀－啭
顠－颥
躊－踌
躋－跻
躑－踯
躍－跃
纍－累
蠟－蜡
囂－嚣
巋－岿
髒－脏

【丿】

儺－傩
儷－俪
儼－俨
鷂－鹞
鐵－铁
鑊－镬
鐳－镭
鐺－铛
鐸－铎

鐶－镮
鐲－镯
鐮－镰
鐿－镱
鷸－鹬
鷗－鸥
雞－鸡
鶬－鸧
臘－腊
䲢－䲢
鰭－鳍
鰱－鲢
鰣－鲥
鰨－鳎
鰥－鳏
鰷－鲦
鰟－鳑
鰜－鳒

【丶】

癲－癫
癥－症
癮－瘾
斕－斓
辯－辩
礱－䃺
鶼－鹣
爛－烂
鶯－莺
灄－滠
灃－沣
灘－滩

囁－慑
懼－惧
竈－灶
顧－顾
襯－衬
鶴－鹤

【一】

屬－属
纈－缬
續－续
纏－缠

22 劃

【一】

鬚－须
驍－骁
驕－骄
攤－摊
覿－觌
攢－攒
鷙－鸷
聽－听
蘿－萝
驚－惊
轢－轹
鷗－鸥
鑒－鉴
邐－逦
鷥－鹭
霽－霁

【丨】

齵－齬	鰾－鳔	驗－验	鱒－鳟
齺－齼	鱈－鳕	攬－揽	鱘－鲟
鱉－鳖	鰻－鳗	欏－椤	【、】
贖－赎	鱅－鳙	轤－轳	讞－谳
躪－躏	鰼－鳛	厴－厣	欒－栾
躓－踬	玀－猡	魘－魇	攣－挛
蠱－蟓	【、】	曆－餍	變－变
蘇－苏	讀－读	鷃－鹌	戀－恋
囉－啰	譸－诪	鼶－鼶	鷟－鸑
囒－㘎	巒－峦	顪－颥	癱－瘫
輾－辗	彎－弯	【丨】	齏－齑
巔－巅	攣－李	曬－晒	讐－雠
巖－岩	變－变	鷉－鹧	【一】
邏－逻	顫－颤	顯－显	鸊－鹈
體－体	鷗－鸥	蠱－蛊	纓－缨
【丿】	癭－瘿	髖－髋	纖－纤
罎－坛	癬－癣	髕－髌	纔－才
籜－箨	聾－聋	【丿】	鷥－鸶
籟－籁	龔－龚	籤－签	
籙－箓	襲－袭	䲵－雠	**24 劃**
籠－笼	灘－滩	鷦－鹪	【一】
鱉－鳖	灑－洒	黴－霉	鬢－鬓
儻－傥	竊－窃	鑠－铄	攬－揽
艫－舻	【一】	鑕－锧	驟－骤
鑄－铸	鷚－鹨	鑪－镥	壩－坝
鑌－镔	彎－㐷	鑛－镳	韆－千
鑔－镲		鑭－镧	觀－观
龕－龛	**23 劃**	臢－臜	鹽－盐
糴－籴	【一】	鱖－鳜	釀－酿
鋤－耡	瓆－瓒	鱔－鳝	靂－雳
鰹－鲣	驛－驿	鱗－鳞	靈－灵

靆 – 霭
蠶 – 蚕

【丨】

艷 – 艳
礬 – 矾
齲 – 龋
齷 – 龌
礆 – 碱
贜 – 赃
鷥 – 鹭
囑 – 嘱
羈 – 羁

【丿】

籩 – 笾
籬 – 篱
籪 – 簖
黌 – 黉
鱟 – 鲎
鱠 – 鲙
鱣 – 鳣

【丶】

讕 – 谰
讖 – 谶
讒 – 谗
讓 – 让
鸇 – 鹯
鷹 – 鹰
癱 – 瘫
癲 – 癫
贛 – 赣

灝 – 灏

【一】

鷿 – 鹏

25 劃

【一】

韉 – 鞯
欖 – 榄
靉 – 叆

【丨】

顱 – 颅
躚 – 跹
躦 – 躜
黿 – 鼋

【丿】

籮 – 箩
鑭 – 镧
鑰 – 钥
鑲 – 镶
饞 – 馋
鱨 – 鲿
鱭 – 鲚

【丶】

蠻 – 蛮
廧 – 裔
廳 – 厅
灣 – 湾

【一】

糶 – 粜
纘 – 缵

26 劃

【一】

驥 – 骥
驢 – 驴
趲 – 趱
顴 – 颧
厴 – 厣
釃 – 酾
釀 – 酿

【丨】

矚 – 瞩
躪 – 躏
躓 – 踬

【丿】

釁 – 衅
鑷 – 镊
鑹 – 镩

【丶】

灤 – 滦

27 劃

【一】

鬮 – 阄
纕 – 瓤
顳 – 颞

【丨】

鸕 – 鸬
黷 – 黩

【丿】

鑼 – 锣

鑽 – 钻
鱸 – 鲈

【丶】

讜 – 谠
讞 – 谳
鑾 – 銮
灧 – 滟

【一】

纜 – 缆

28 劃

鸛 – 鹳
櫺 – 棂
鑿 – 凿
鸚 – 鹦
鑭 – 锐
钁 – 镢
戇 – 戆

29 劃

驪 – 骊
鬱 – 郁

30 劃

鸝 – 鹂
饢 – 馕
鱺 – 鲡
鸞 – 鸾

32 劃

籲 – 吁